A VERY
POLITICAL
RAILWAY

To Daisy

A VERY POLITICAL RAILWAY

The fight for the North London Line
1945–2014

Wayne Asher

First published 2014
ISBN 978-1-85414-378-5

© Wayne Asher 2014

Published by Capital Transport Publishing Ltd
www.capitaltransport.com

Printed by Parksons Graphics

CONTENTS

1970s – advertising the line in the form of a beer mat.

A note on abbreviations

BR	British Railways, or, post 1965, British Rail	Rail operating arm of the BRB
BRB	British Railways Board	Statutory corporation, responsible to the transport ministry for the entire railway network
BRPB	British Railways Property Board	Arm of the BRB responsible for realising the railways' vast property assets some of which resulted from line closures
DLR	Docklands Light Railway	
ELLE	East London Line Extension	The proposed extension of the line northwards to Dalston
ELLG	East London Line Group	Lobby group – funded by business and local authorities – which helped keep ELLE on the political agenda
ER	Eastern Region	Successor to the pre-nationalisation LNER and responsible inter alia for the Great Northern lines from King's Cross and for the North London Line east of Dalston. Superseded in 1982 by the London & South East sector.
GLA	Greater London Assembly	An elected body that scrutinises the activities of the Mayor of London
GLC	Greater London Council	London's elected strategic authority – formed 1965 and abolished 1986
HAPTAC	Hackney Public Transport Action Committee	Pressure group which campaigned for better transport in a (then) tubeless borough
HLOS	High Level Output Specification	The government's high-level plans for rail projects and spending
HS2	High Speed 2	The proposed high speed line from Euston to Birmingham
LDDC	London Docklands Development Commission	Unelected body set up by the Thatcher government in 1981 to kickstart the stalled regeneration of Docklands
LMR	London Midland Region	Successor to the pre-nationalisation LMSR and responsible for the North London Line west of Dalston until superseded in 1982 by the London & South East sector.
LMSR	London Midland & Scottish Railway	Successor to the LNWR which became the LMR of British Railways after nationalisation in 1948

LOROL	London Overground Rail Operations Limited	The concessionaire running the Overground lines on behalf of TfL
LRPC	London Regional Passengers' Committee	Successor to the London TUCC from 1984 to 2000. Replaced by London Travelwatch
LSE	London & South East sector	Formed 1982 to bring all BR lines in London under one strategic control instead of being split among the old regions
LT	London Transport	
LUL	London Underground Limited	Set up after the GLC was abolished and responsible, through London Regional Transport, to the transport secretary. Subsumed into TfL in 2000
LNWR	London & North Western Railway	Merged into LMSR in 1923 and the owner of the original North London Railway
NLL	North London Line	
NLLC	North London Line Committee	Pressure group set up in 1971 which campaigned for better services
NLR	North London Railway	The original company
NLR	North London Railways	With an 's'.....the shadow franchise in place from 1994 to 1997 when the line was operated on a private enterprise basis before being moved to a fully franchised basis
NORP	North Orbital Rail Partnership	TfL sponsored alliance of local councils served by the North London Line and which worked on station improvements from 2005 to 2011
NSE	Network SouthEast	Created 1986 as branding for the London & South East sector
NSWJ	North & South Western Joint Railway	The stretch of line linking Willesden Junction with Kew Bridge, which became the western section of the North London Line
PFI	Private Finance Initiative	Controversial project finance method devised in 1992 and which involved private finance in public sector projects. Regarded by its opponents as being very bad value for money
PiXC	Passengers in Excess of Capacity	A post privatisation measure of overcrowding
PLA	Port of London Authority	

PPM	Public Performance Measure	A post privatisation measure of train operator reliability and punctuality
PPP	Public-Private Partnership	Contract between a public authority and a private sector body where the latter should be taking a measure of risk
RUS	Route Utilisation Strategy	A strategic look at a part of the rail network, its usage and capability in relation to current and future demand
SRA	Strategic Rail Authority	Set up under the 1997 Labour government to provide strategic direction and regulation to the fragmented railway network post privatisation. Abolished 2006
T&H	Tottenham & Hampstead Joint	Railway that links Gospel Oak with Barking via Tottenham. A key freight route but with a passenger service which also survived the Beeching axe
TfL	Transport for London	Responsible for all of London Transport and created in 2000 following the creation of the post of directly elected Mayor for London
TUCC	Transport Users Consultative Committee	Set up by the 1947 Transport Act to represent passengers' interests. Replaced in 1984 by the London Regional Passengers' Committee
TWA	Transport and Works Act	Since 1992 an order made under the Act is the usual way of authorising a rail scheme in England and Wales

PREFACE

This is the story of the North London Line – London's only real cross-town rail route, which serves eight boroughs in just 16 miles.

It is the story of the line since the Second World War, how it was threatened with closure under the Beeching axe and how it was allowed to decay before being transformed into a key part of the up-to-the-minute London Overground network.

We will try to see not just what happened but why the key decisions were made, regardless of what the public were told at the time. In such a tale, rich in social history and political controversy, the reader will expect to encounter heroes and villains – and both will be found. But the railway managers responsible for an unreliable and sometimes dangerously overcrowded service do not, by and large, figure among them. They were just trying to run the best service they could with the resources they were given. It is even debatable to what degree Dr Beeching should figure among the villains. He raised serious questions about what a railway was for, where it should concentrate its strengths, and his analysis of freight traffic proved to be spot on and in many ways well ahead of his time.

For real villains we must instead look to the politicians – those who, despite all the evidence to the contrary, tried to make a public service into a profit-making enterprise based on mass line closures, and appointed Dr Beeching to carry out this plan; those who then underfunded the railways in the 1960s, 70s and 80s, before selling them off to the highest bidder in the 90s. All the evils besetting the North London Line for so long can – and should – be laid at their door. The railwaymen just managed the results.

As for heroes, they too are easily discernable: first and absolutely foremost, those private individuals who fought long and hard to save the line from closure in the 1960s and again in the 1970s. These small groups of dedicated and committed people had an influence far beyond their numbers.

Then there are Ken Livingstone and the Greater London Council leadership who had a vision of cheap and reliable public transport in the capital.

There are even unlikely heroes to be found among the national politicians. John Peyton, the Tory transport minister under Ted Heath who had the courage to admit that Labour had a better grasp of railway funding than his own party. And Alistair Darling, transport secretary under Tony Blair and chancellor under Gordon Brown, who overcame New Labour's dislike of Livingstone to hand over control of the North London Line to his team in 2006, a far sighted act which led to a railway revolution in the capital.

Passengers, politicians, railwaymen; they all share the history which follows.

OVERTURE

In which we look at some ancient history … you can't, after all, understand the present without understanding at least a little of the past.

The North London Line had, in its inception, precious little to do with north London or the needs of its citizens at all. Instead it arose from the desire of the mighty London and North Western Railway (LNWR), the largest railway in Victorian Britain, to get a rail link to the London Docks, and the complicated story of the various companies which became the North London requires a brief summary in order that modern history makes sense.

An Act to allow the building of the East and West India Docks and Birmingham Junction Railway became law in August 1846, for a railway to be built from Camden to Blackwall. Nominally independent, it was, in practice completely controlled by the LNWR.

It opened – in the midst of an economic slump – from Islington to Bow Junction, allowing passenger trains to run into Fenchurch Street in 1850, and extended to the junction with the LNWR at Camden in 1851, and at the other end, to Poplar Dock, which became the first railway-owned dock in the capital.

This incredibly circuitous route to the City was a serious handicap, and in 1865, the expensive link from Dalston to a brand new terminus at Broad Street was opened. It required the building of a long viaduct and destruction of 4,500 people's homes. Passenger traffic doubled as a result – but overcrowding increased in the slum neighbourhoods affected.

In 1853 another piece of the jigsaw fell into place in west London, linking the LNWR at Willesden with the London and South Western Railway at Kew Bridge. This was the North and South Western Junction Railway (NSWJ), and passenger trains on this were worked by the North London from the outset, providing a service from Broad Street to Kew.

This traffic added to the congestion on the LNWR main line between Willesden and Camden. So a new line from Camden, via Hampstead Heath and including a three-quarter mile tunnel under the Heath and on to high-level platforms at Willesden, was opened in 1860. It was worked by the North London but owned outright by the LNWR. From 1869 North London trains began to run to Richmond.

Only from 1916 – as a wartime measure – was the line at Gospel Oak connected to the Tottenham & Hampstead Joint (T&H) line which ran via South Tottenham and Walthamstow to Barking. This was to prove a major freight link.

Soon North London trains would run to the northern heights too. The Great Northern Railway (GNR), which considered itself a long distance route to Yorkshire and the north, had a fast growing suburban traffic which caused headaches in the congested stretch south of Finsbury Park. So the GN built a line from Finsbury Park to join the North London – the Canonbury Curve – originally to run freight trains to its own goods depot at Poplar Dock. The GNR applied for permission to run suburban passenger trains to Broad Street, so taking some strain off King's Cross. The LNWR vetoed this and in desperation the GNR agreed to North London trains running out to the northern heights suburbs.

The critical point to remember in all this is that we are talking about a horse drawn, gas-lit, pre-tube world. The Hampstead tube only opened in 1907, the same year that electric tramways reached Hampstead and Stamford Hill. So for several decades the North London was by far the quickest way for much of north and west London to reach the City, and for a time, Broad Street was London's second busiest station (second only to Liverpool Street).

It boasted eight – later nine – platforms, and trains ran to Poplar via Hackney and Victoria Park, Richmond, Kew Bridge, Watford, Mansion House via Willesden, Earl's Court, and the District Line (the Outer Circle), plus suburban trains to Edgware, Barnet and Hertford.

By 1874, the demands of freight traffic had justified building four tracks between Broad Street and Camden.

The railway had carried 32 million passengers in 1880 and 49 million by 1896. But tramway and tube competition soon offered faster and more direct routes, and slaughtered passenger traffic, which fell to 21 million in 1913 and just 11 million by 1921.

In 1909 the North London surrendered operating control to the LNWR with no guarantee of dividends being paid to its shareholders. The LNWR's vision was to electrify these lines as the only way to fight off competition. Electric trains, running on a third and fourth rail DC system, duly started to Richmond in 1916 and between Willesden and Earl's Court, and to Watford in 1922. The service to Poplar remained steam hauled.

The LNWR took full control in 1922, a year before that company became part of the London Midland and Scottish Railway (LMSR).

The LMSR made few changes. Mildmay Park station between Canonbury and Dalston closed in 1934, but it was the Second World War which really forced change on the line. The service to Kew Bridge was shut in 1940 as was the electric service from Willesden to Earl's Court. Haggerston station closed in 1940 and Shoreditch followed soon after. Victoria Park station went in 1943 and the entire service to war-devastated Poplar – where bombing left 18 per cent of the borough's land derelict – was ended on 23 April 1945.

From here, our main story can begin.

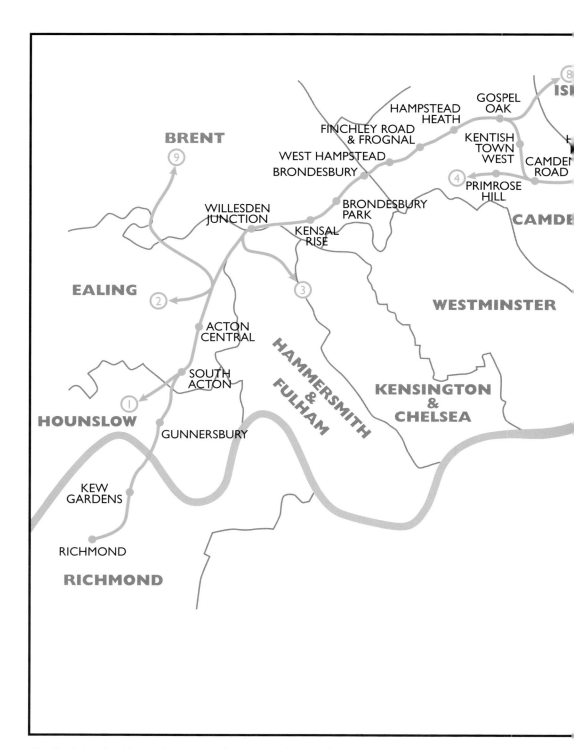

The North London Line and its connections set against London's borough boundaries.

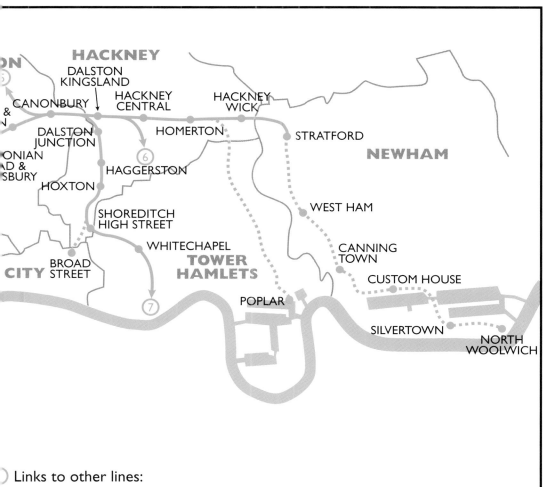

Links to other lines:
- Kew Bridge and Southern lines
- Western Region lines
- West London Line to Clapham Junction
- Watford Junction and West Coast Main Line
- Canonbury Curve to Great Northern line
- Graham Road Curve to Liverpool Street
- East London Line to New Cross
- Gospel Oak to Barking line
- Dudding Hill loop to Midland Main Line

otted lines show abandoned connections

Drawn by Mike Harris

1945–1960: PICKING UP THE PIECES

In which we look at the state of the North London Line after the war, and examine official resistance to reopening services closed during the conflict

The post war period saw the North London Line in a poor state. Some stations had been heavily bombed and there was no money to repair them, while the trains themselves, some dating from 1916, were life expired. However the rest of the railway network was in a similar state, as indeed was the entire country, which had been bankrupted by the war effort. The grey and miserable state of the nation is well captured in the black and white films of the era.

Not surprisingly, the line, which at least offered an electrically hauled service to its customers, rather than a filthy steam operated one, did not rank high in the priority list for scarce post-war resources.

State ownership from 1948 actually began with three pieces of unfinished business to sort out. All concerned services which had been cut back during the war as emergency measures.

The service from Broad Street to Poplar had been suspended in 1944 – a week before D Day – and closed 'until further notice' in April 1945. But it was technically still in limbo. In 1947, there was agitation from employers in the Hackney Wick area for it to be restored. The Railway Executive, probably with the needs of freight from the docks in mind, claimed that reopening the often bomb damaged stations would cost £72,000. The area served had suffered badly from bombing and population was falling. The Executive was advised that there was no legal difficulty standing in the way of permanent closure, and that indeed, 'there would appear to be no demand' for restoration. Shoreditch, Haggerston, Hackney, Homerton, Victoria Park, Old Ford, Bow, South Bromley and Poplar (East India Road) were, therefore, formally closed in 1949.

However it wasn't quite true that 'there was no demand' for the service; in 1951 Hackney and Poplar borough councils jointly approached BR asking for the service to be restored, only to be rebuffed. A similar proposal in 1957 from the Railway Development Society also got nowhere.

When it came to the Acton Central to Kew Bridge service, a 5 February 1950 LMR recommendation to the British Transport Commission said there was little prospect of attracting increased traffic to rail by restoring the service. Much traction equipment had already been removed and further recoveries were possible to the value of £2,019.

Referring to possible objections, local councils were to be kept in the dark: 'As the passenger service has not been available for a number of years it is not proposed to communicate with the local authorities' while passenger services could be restored only at the cost of dislocating the heavy freight service. On 21 February 1950, the service was formally withdrawn for an estimated annual saving of £7,162 of which £6,789 was made up of train working expenses, staff costs, and electricity.

The service from Willesden to Earl's Court proved to be a stickier proposition. A huge new government office block – Charles House – had been established close to Olympia, initially for the 5,000 workers at the Post Office Savings Bank (now National Savings). More civil servants were expected to transfer there, and their trade unions agitated for a return of this service, pointing out that without it, their members in north-west London would have to travel into the centre and then out again.

Even before nationalisation, the Standing Joint Committee, meeting on 20 June 1947, had ruled out a return of this service, ruling that prospects for development of passenger traffic were poor as there was little affinity between the north-west and south-west districts, adding that 'These railways must be regarded as primarily for the use of freight traffic'.

After nationalisation this remained the consistent position; local people were not to be considered the major stakeholders for this group of railways, although this fact was rarely spelt out quite this clearly. On 2 September 1949, the Civil Service Clerical Association raised the issue with the Transport Users Consultative Committee (TUCC). But on 11 October the TUCC turned the civil servants down, saying priority had to be given to freight, an answer repeated a year later, and this negative response was again repeated in October 1950.

However during the 1950s, NLL passengers seem to have been a reasonably happy lot – the minutes of the London TUCC, set up after the railways were nationalised, showed no complaints or even representations from local councils over inadequate services. The TUCC business during this period was dominated to a remarkable extent by the concerns of outer London.

Freight traffic, especially from the docks, remained heavy. But passenger traffic on the line fell after the introduction of new fares in March 1952. The British Transport Commission controversially changed the basis of fares so that the same charge per mile was applied to everyone in similar circumstances. Previously there had been a number of fare scales below this, with the result that passengers paying the ordinary fares were subsidising those paying lower fares, essentially those travelling on early morning and season ticket fares.

There were other small whispers in the wind that that line as it stood had a problematic future. Late in 1948 the British Transport Hotels' executive recommended that the Broad Street refreshment room be closed. It employed 40–50 staff but the only viable trade was at lunchtime. 'The reputation of the rooms attracts a large clientele from City business workers,' reported Lord Inman of the BTH executive, but even so it had lost money every year since 1946. It was thought that refreshment facilities gave an indirect boost to rail traffic – so it was decided to see if private enterprise could do better.

Bertram & Co took on the lease, but with little more success, its tenancy being punctuated by a complaint to BR in October 1956 about water leaks and plaster falls narrowly missing customers.

It was a hopeless proposition and Bertram & Co gave up, the room closing on 1 June 1963. Two ugly brick structures had already been built on the concourse at Broad Street to provide ticket facilities and toilets, and these in turn made it possible to close other parts of the building.

However a start was made on rebuilding some of the decaying and war damaged stations, with Willesden High Level, Hampstead Heath and Gospel Oak all acquiring new structures in 1952–1957. It isn't clear why just these three were rebuilt while the rest continued to moulder. The High Level platform at Willesden Junction featured wide steel canopies, staff accommodation and a small waiting room. If the view over the main line and the adjoining depot was hardly beautiful, the station felt pleasant enough to use and was a good example of 1950s' architecture, while the wide canopies provided excellent shelter from the elements. As part of the work at Willesden, the old West London Line platform at the High Level platforms was demolished.

Gospel Oak was rebuilt in 1955 in a simple but pleasant post-war austerity style, with a clean brick double height ticket office at street level, and ample canopy protection for passengers on the platforms. This station remains in use today with little change apart from the addition of lifts to the platforms.

Modernisation of the island platform building, and other alterations, were completed at Highbury & Islington in 1956.

In 1953, that is, before the ill-fated BR 1955 Modernisation Plan, it was decided to completely renew the rolling stock for the line, after the chief carriage and wagon engineer complained that the ex-LNWR Oerlikon[1] stock was life expired. Much of 1954 was spent in working out the design – the London Midland Region (LMR) civil engineer vetoed BR standard stock because of the reduced clearance in Hampstead Tunnel.

It was decided to build 57 three-car electric units based on the Southern Region's 4-EPB class. Fully laden they could accommodate 257 passengers.

Because of the clearance issue, the three coaches were – at 57 feet each – somewhat shorter that the normal length of Southern trains, and had a motor coach, with open seating, a centre compartment car, and finally a trailer car, again with open seating. There were five seats in two rows with a luggage net above. The window droplights were fitted with bars preventing the passengers leaning out of the window, a precaution made necessary by the narrow clearance in Hampstead Tunnel.

Unlike Southern stock, the new units featured a destination blind, and at the centre of each end, there was space for the two digit numerical code characteristic of the Southern Region.

---

1   Named after the Swiss firm which built it.

Brondesbury station before the 'minimal facilities' of the late 1960s.

These headcodes were designed for the benefit of signal staff, and their decoding appeared in the working timetable, but never in the public one. The main codes used were B1 for Euston to Watford, B2 for Broad Street to Watford and B4 for Broad Street to Richmond. The combination of the destination blinds, headcodes and barred windows made these units emblematic of the North London Line.

They were slam-door stock, whereas the old Oerlikon stock had sliding doors. (Although the ex-LMSR stock which shared services on the line also had slam doors.) And there was some grumbling from first class passengers in particular whose sumptuous accommodation vanished with the new units as no first class accommodation was provided.[2]

The first of the new trains did not come into service until 27 May 1957 due to delays in getting steel for the underframes from Round Oak steelworks near Wolverhampton.

Within five years, cutbacks in the service had already made some of these units surplus to requirements, and storm clouds were gathering over the line itself.

---

2   *Railway Magazine*, August 1957.

1962–1965:
'THIS TROUBLESOME MATTER'

In which we look at how well-organised protest saved the line from the Beeching axe, and how the authorities worked to conceal the truth about the closure from passengers.

The opening shots in the battle for the North London Line came early, predating the Beeching report and its call for massive line closures, including so-called duplicate main lines as well as rural branches.

In March 1962, faced with the impact TV was having on evening leisure travel, the basic service was cut from two three-car sets to one only, which meant a saving on electricity costs, although six-car trains still ran on a few peak hour services. Then, from 10 September, the LMR scrapped the late evening service, with the last train now leaving Broad Street at 8.58pm instead of 10.58 and from Richmond at 9.00pm instead of 11.05. This cutback was a serious disincentive to using the line for evening leisure travel. You could certainly go out, but not get home again without a level of inconvenience.

Richmond Borough Council protested to BR, which replied that the point of the exercise was to save on staff costs. By ending the service at 9pm, the entire line could be managed with just two crew shifts instead of three. BR explained to a protest delegation from Brentford & Chiswick Borough Council that this cut had made 'substantial savings' and the only alternative would have been to have a break in service during the day. Richmond retorted that the root of the problems with the North London Line lay in 'lack of publicity' and 'uncompetitive charges'. From the same date, the off-peak service frequency was cut from every 15 minutes to every 20 minutes.

On 7 January 1963, the peak hour service frequency was also cut from every 15 minutes to every 20 minutes, and the London Transport Users Consultative Committee (TUCC) heard at its meeting on 31 January of 'strong local rumours' that BR wanted to shut the line completely.

The Beeching report – *The Reshaping of British Railways* – was published on 27 March 1963. It listed the North London Line for closure to passenger services – one of only a handful of closures proposed in the capital.[3]

Beeching's closure proposal applied only to the Broad Street – Richmond service; the half hourly Broad Street to Watford service was to be 'modified', but there was no proposal to shut the stations on this stretch (Camden Road to Broad Street).

---

3   The others included Kentish Town to Barking, and Clapham Junction to Kensington Olympia. Surprisingly, but relevant to the continuing story, the Docklands branch from Stratford to North Woolwich escaped.

Beeching: chasing the profitable Railway.

The Reshaping of British Railways contained no closure dates; these had to be raised by the individual railway regions and follow the closure process laid down in the 1962 Transport Act. There was, therefore, time to organise and mobilise local opposition.

Within a few weeks no fewer than eight local action committees sprang up to fight closure – in Hackney, Islington, St Pancras, Hampstead, Willesden, Acton, Brentford & Chiswick, and Richmond. They were coordinated through a Joint Committee run by Christopher Hall, a civil servant who also chaired the Hampstead Committee, and by councillor Pat Waddison of St Pancras, himself a railwayman and an activist in the National Union of Railwaymen. Protest meetings drew large crowds: 300 at Hampstead Town Hall, 250 in Chiswick and another 200 at a town meeting in Willesden.

Richmond-Broad Street Line
PROTEST MEETING
AT CHISWICK

Headline and extract from newspaper report of a protest meeting being held on 23 September 1963.

THE Brentford and Chiswick committee of the " Save the Broad Street/Richmond Line Campaign," have arranged a public protest meeting at Chiswick Town Hall next Wednesday, September 23, at 8 p.m.

Dr. Beeching has declined an invitation to attend. In his letter to local committee secretary Mrs. E. Tendler the railways chief says, " the issues involved are such that it is unlikely that they can be clarified sufficiently for a decision to be made and announced until the end of the year."

If as a result of the meeting next Wednesday the committee wishes to add anything to the representations already made on behalf of the users, Dr. Beeching says they will " no doubt inform the LMR general manager so that he can take it into consideration in his review of the issues involved."

Dr. Beeching says the committee " will appreciate that I could not wish to appear at a public meeting to speak on a matter which, while it is under consideration, is the responsibility of the Region concerned."

Opposition to a line closure was normal. But the North London was different from the typical Beeching closure proposal; it was no poorly patronised branch line which really was hopelessly uneconomic but a well-used service providing the only orbital route across the capital.

Under pressure, on 7 December, British Railways announced that a closure decision would be postponed. This was a mixed blessing. On one hand, it provided more time to marshal opposition but it also meant more time for passengers to drift away and less time to start promotional activities to encourage usage.

The records of the Hampstead committee survive, and show that a cadre of 15 to 20 people maintained a two-year long campaign, organising a series of public meetings, gathering material for objections for when a formal closure proposal finally arrived, conducting their own census of traffic, and even producing a film about the line. They had wide support in the borough, ranging from the local Communist Party to Geoffrey Finsberg, a local councillor who eventually became Conservative MP for Hampstead.

Just like Richmond Borough Council the previous year, the committee argued that the line was not intrinsically uneconomic – it 'could pay its way if it were more efficiently run and advertised', and to make the point it distributed 5,000 timetables locally to get people to use the line.

It was striking that the campaign to save the North London Line sustained itself for over two years with such a high level of activity and organisation.

Support from local authorities was important; in St Pancras, the council provided town hall facilities plus a grant towards legal advice. In Brentford & Chiswick the council actually instigated the launch of the local action group. It provided funding and allowed free use of Chiswick Town Hall for meetings. Hampstead council provided first a £50 grant, and then a further £195 to pay for the printing of a 52-page booklet – *Hampstead and the Broad Street Line* – which was a professionally produced, closely argued case for the service to be retained, stressing the fact that it was uneconomic only because it was not properly run and advertised by British Railways' management.

The Guardian couldn't resist calling it a 'cogent 50-page pamphlet by Hampstead intellectuals' – but its review was very sympathetic.[4] There was interest elsewhere too, and a request from the Transport ministry's library to be added to the Hampstead committee's mailing list survives.

The committee pointed to the poor and uninviting quality of the stations themselves as deterring passengers, an issue we will return to later. They also complained that the BR fare structure discriminated against the North London Line because it was mileage based, so passengers on a fast but somewhat circuitous route paid more than on competing London Transport lines.

A ticket from Finchley Road to Broad Street, a 22-minute journey, cost 2s 0d, whereas a journey from Finchley Road Metropolitan Line to Liverpool Street, which took 22 or 29 minutes, only cost 1s 6d. A journey from Hampstead Heath to Broad Street (20 minutes) cost 1s 9d, whereas one from nearby Belsize Park on the Northern Line to the City cost only 1s 3d.

London Transport came in for sharp criticism for refusing to include the line on the tube map. LT argued that inclusion would only prompt similar demands from other surface lines. Members even mystery-shopped LT's travel advisory services and proved that passengers asking for journey information were not told about the North London Line even when it was the quickest and cheapest route – Finchley Road to Kew Gardens, or Dalston to Hampstead for example.

There were no through fares between the line and London Transport, while car parking was not available even when, at Gospel Oak (for example) there was derelict railway land available to provide it.

At this time it was a popular suggestion that the North London Line should be transferred to London Transport, but the Hampstead committee didn't support this, on the principled grounds that if the line were unprofitable for British Railways it would be equally unprofitable for London Transport, and that the real point was to improve matters so it became profitable.

The committee was tireless. It complained to BR management about the

4   *The Guardian*, 30 April 1964.

non-existent evening service, as well as the severe overcrowding on three peak hour trains to Broad Street. (Leslie Leppington, the LMR's London divisional manager at Euston, subsequently denied that there was a particular problem.)

Then there was pure incompetence, as on the occasion at Easter 1964 when the railways ran extra trains to cater for homeward bound passengers from Hampstead Heath – and failed to advertise the fact on the station itself.

Interestingly, the Hampstead Committee demonstrated from its own census work that most traffic was not – as might have been expected – made up of well-off bankers travelling to the City but was far more widely distributed. Arrivals at Hampstead Heath in May 1963 showed only 15 per cent were City commuters coming from Broad Street. Fourteen per cent came from Dalston and the three Islington stations, 22 per cent from Finchley Road and West End Lane, 11 per cent from the three stations in Camden, and the balance from West Hampstead westwards to Richmond.

Middle-class Hampstead wasn't unique in its ability to run and sustain this kind of campaign – the fight against closure was as strong in working class Willesden, where the organisational structures needed to elect officers, keep minutes, run committee meetings, and manage finance were well understood by the many people involved in the trades union movement.

The campaign to save the line made it to television on ITV's *Here and Now* programme on 5 May 1964, which interviewed Christopher Hall and Henry 'Bill' Johnson, the LMR's general manager. The presenter noted that 'at Canonbury, the name of the station is still blanked out to confuse spies and invaders … shrapnel marks and twisted girders dominate the scene'.

The joint committee organised a lobby of Parliament on 13 May 1963, with 300 people attending the protest meeting there, including seven MPs and the mayors of Richmond, Willesden and Hackney. They presented a petition signed by 57,000 people, and got the issue raised in Parliament on several occasions.

As a railwayman, Pat Waddison was able to cultivate sources of information from within BR itself. In June 1964 he began to pick up rumours that BR was also planning to close the DC electrified services from Watford into Euston and Broad Street. British Railways refused to confirm or deny this, but in October, Waddison was able to drop a bombshell, when he claimed that internal BR figures showed that the loss on the North London Line passenger services had fallen to just £12,000 a year.

BR refused to provide up to date figures, and £12,000 was totally irreconcilable with BR's earlier figures given that nothing had changed. Hall scoffed that the losses on the line were clearly 'of the bookkeeping variety, which any competent accountant can create or abolish at will'.

The joint committee carefully built relations with MPs along the line, several of whom, especially Anthony Royle (Conservative, Richmond), Dudley Smith (Conservative, Brentford & Chiswick) and Laurie Pavitt (Labour, Willesden) were central to the campaign

The first Commons debate was instigated by Laurie Pavitt on 17 May 1963. He asked for the line to be treated as a special case: 'I am making a special plea this afternoon. This is not the ordinary argument against the whole Report. I am not arguing Beeching. I am not arguing transport. I am making a special plea for the 14 Members of the House whose constituents use this service.' Transport minister Ernest Marples, the motorway magnate who appointed Beeching to force through mass line closures at BR, was present and stonewalled. He set the tone for all ministerial comments on the line for the next two years: 'I must ask this question: what ought I to say about this case? Quite frankly, the answer is "Nothing." All opposed passenger closures will come to me for decision. Each case will go through the same statutory procedure and will be handled in the same way. Each will be looked at on its merits with the greatest care. That is all I can say now about the Richmond – Broad Street line.'

Ernest Marples, who appointed Dr Beeching.

By October 1964 power had changed. Labour was in office and Marples was no longer the transport minister. Yet Labour was secretly planning to renege on its election commitment to halt line closures, and the new set of ministers continued to stall. On 11 November, Royle asked for an assurance that if the new minister received a closure proposal he would turn it down. Stephen Swingler, speaking for the new transport minister, Tom Fraser, replied: 'I should have thought that there is no great uncertainty about this line, because there is as yet no proposal to withdraw the service'.

This was the constant reply given to objectors. Just as it was under Marples. Closure questions were for the BRB not for ministers, and as no formal closure proposal had been put forward there was, therefore, nothing for them to decide.

On 11 December 1964 Royle was back in action. The North London Line was already becoming slightly embarrassing for the new Labour government – several successful Labour candidates in the area had campaigned on the future of the line at the October election, but it seemed that nothing had changed.

Royle read from a letter from Dr Beeching dated 7 May 1964, in which the latter wrote, 'It is true that last October the LMR stated that it would be about six months before a decision would be taken whether to proceed with the proposal to withdraw this service or not. Time was needed to study the effect of the economy measures which had been introduced since the publication of *Reshaping*, and of others which were in mind at the time. This is a much more complicated question than the average passenger train withdrawal proposal. It has to be considered in relation both to other services using Broad Street station and to railway planning for the future'.

Swingler tried hard to help the board, saying: 'In fairness to the board, it is understandable that it should take a longer time to formulate a definite proposal since it differs considerably from the much smaller branch lines about which proposals have been put up. The board has now told me that it hopes to reach a definite conclusion within the next month or so'. It didn't.

When Bernard Floud (Labour, Acton) asked on 11 February 1965 for an update he was told by Tom Fraser: 'The board has not yet put any proposals to me. I understand that it is still examining possible ways of maintaining an economic service. I hope to have its proposals before very long'. On 28 April he gave the same reply to Dudley Smith: 'I have received no proposals ... about the Richmond – Broad Street line. The board announced on 24 February that it was continuing its investigations to try to find more economic ways of running the service. It is my hope that these investigations will yield a solution acceptable to all concerned'.

Royle did not give up. He won a third adjournment debate on 4 June 1965. This time he complained bitterly about 'the shabby story of broken faith with the electorate and the House of Commons', pointing to pledges made during the General Election campaign that an incoming Labour government would remove the threat.

Swingler stalled yet again: 'Let me repeat that no proposal has been made to the minister of transport and therefore, since the publication of the Beeching report, it has not fallen to the minister of transport to take any decision whatsoever about this line'. Swingler desperately tried to go on the offensive pointing out, reasonably enough, that it was the Tories who had insisted that the railways must pay their way in the first place. 'Yet,' he retorted, 'We have a queue of Tory members asking the minister of transport for heavy subsidies for their lightly used lines and stations.'

The 1962 Transport Act had been carefully framed to hobble effective opposition to railway closures. It did not allow objectors to query the accuracy or otherwise of the figures British Railways provided. They could only object on the grounds of hardship to passengers. This was a serious obstacle in the way of communities faced with the loss of their railway service, and this Catch 22 boosted suspicions that British Railways were not above cooking the books in order to force closures through.

The figures BR provided to the London Transport Users Consultative Committee (TUCC) for the North London Line were as follows:

Table one – BR closure figures 1963

REVENUE	£	EXPENSES	£
Direct earnings	245,000	Movement	135,000
Contributory gross revenue	280,000	Terminals	191,000
=	525,000	=	326,000
Revenue expected to be retained after closure	254,000	Direct signalling and track expenses	14,000
NET LOSS	271,000	Total gain through reduced expenses at closure	340,000

That meant that closing the line would save the railways £69,000 a year (£340,000 - £271,000) – or approximately £1.2 million in today's money, a figure the Hampstead committee thought 'pathetic.' The figures were certainly odd. Among the unanswered questions were:

- How did BR expect to retain half the revenue after closure? All experience was that after closure passengers simply took the bus or bought a car and were lost to the railways for good.
- What was the contribution of freight revenue to the line? And how would that affect the picture?
- How could savings be made anyway? The trains had already been paid for and only the stations from South Acton to Kentish Town West would be affected by closure. Train movement costs would in any case be reduced when the railway-owned Stonebridge Park power station was shut and power taken from the national grid.

For *Hampstead and the Broad Street Line*, the Hampstead committee got Neil Rubra, a professional economist, to come up with a figure for the social cost of closure – no less than £578,000 a year. In the world of Marples and Beeching this figure was irrelevant. The railway either paid its way or it didn't. Yet the Conservative government had explicitly factored in these cost/benefits – essentially the monetary value of time saved by passengers – when they agreed to build the Victoria Line. Strictly interpreted, this was expected to incur a £2 million a year operating loss, but when social benefits were included, mainly the impact on traffic congestion, the new tube would easily justify itself.

It is true that many of the figures used to justify rail closures were valid – *The Reshaping of British Railways* revealed that half the entire network was only carrying four per cent of passenger traffic and five per cent of freight, while a third of the 4,300 stations accounted for less than one per cent of revenue. (The 34 largest stations accounted for 26 per cent.)

Many but not all though. As Gerard Fiennes, the independent-minded general manager of the Eastern Region, pointed out, the fact that a line lost money today didn't mean that it was doomed to do so for ever. Better management, more efficient working and cost cutting could turn loss into profit, a critical point completely ignored in the Beeching report. (Fiennes' penchant for independent thinking eventually got him the sack in 1967, when he published his experiences and criticisms of BR management in *I Tried to Run a Railway*.)

But was the usage of the North London Line really so bad? The Hampstead committee pointed out that British Railways, and indeed Dr Beeching himself, was often complaining about the poor economics of a peak hour network, where expensively built trains only earned revenue for a few hours each day and spent the rest of the time sitting idly in the siding. In the early 1960s, rail traffic was becoming more and more concentrated in peak periods, and on average, off-peak travel on BR commuter trains was only 20 per cent of the peak hour total. For London Transport the figure was 25 per cent. Yet the cross-town nature of the North London Line meant that off-peak travel was fully 50 per cent of the peak hour total. Its trains were fully utilised all day, and this should have made it one of the most profitable routes in the capital – not material for a closure proposal.

The Hampstead committee thought it was 'more than likely' that BR had ulterior motives driving the closure plan, safe in the knowledge that its figures and assumptions could not be legally challenged. *Hampstead and the Broad Street Line* put these forward tentatively in the absence of any evidence.

The first was that, at the time, the slow loose-coupled freight trains often delayed the passenger service. But Beeching foresaw a shift towards fast fully-braked liner trains whizzing between far flung destinations. Was BR management worried that the passenger trains could get in the way of a new and potentially very lucrative business?

The second stemmed from the fact that they did not trust BR's commitment to the Watford to Broad Street service, whose own revenue figures would worsen dramatically if the Richmond services were to cease. In that situation, lucrative property sales through closing the Dalston to Broad Street section would be 'an enormously profitable operation'.

With possible ulterior motives in mind, it is time to look at what was happening within British Railways and the Ministry of Transport, using files available at the National Archives at Kew. A lot of BR closure files from this era have been destroyed, but quite enough remain to tell the story.

The first we hear of what BR were really thinking comes in a 27 May 1964 minute from Jim Baxter, a senior transport civil servant. This little-known figure was one of the central people in the administration of the Beeching plan. He chaired the transport ministry's Working Party on Passenger Closure Proposals and it was this group which analysed the recommendations from the regional TUCCs, tried to distinguish between what was 'hardship' to passengers and what was merely 'inconvenience', and made the final recommendation on closure to the minister.

Baxter had enquired of the BRB whether it could make some kind of statement on the future of the line by June. He reported back that 'The situation is more complex than merely the assessment of the commercial prospect of the service; it is tangled with the whole future of the lines running into Broad Street and the future of Broad Street itself'. One possibility, he said, was: 'That the board will desire eventually to divert the remaining services into St Pancras …' So by spring 1964 *at the latest*, the men from the Ministry had good insight into what was really going on. It was just the railways' customers who did not.

But as 1964 faded into 1965, the relentless pressure from the action committees on the new government was having an effect in Whitehall. Frustration was growing at the BRB's unwillingness to provide a clear statement of its plans. The new ministers, therefore, had to stall on questions and complaints: all they could do was repeat the mantra that no closure proposal had been raised and until it was so raised, there was nothing for them to decide.

But frustrated or not, the transport civil servants were consistently anxious not to embarrass Dr Beeching. On 6 May 1964, a week before the 13 May presentation of the Joint Committee's petition, another note from Baxter said: 'The board as are anxious as the parliamentary secretary that any statement they should put out should not look as if it were stimulated by the St Pancras councillors and the Labour Party'.

Internally they debated what advice to give Tom Fraser. Charles Scott-Malden, under secretary in the MoT's Railways Group, worried about whether it was fair to take a strong written approach to Dr Beeching when their concerns had not been put verbally when they met with Fred Margetts, the former general manager of the North Eastern Region who Beeching promoted to the BRB to become his right hand man in the closure programme.

Eventually, on 3 February 1965, Fraser wrote to Beeching about the line saying: 'This is somewhat embarrassing to me and I am currently having to answer a stream of questions in the House asking for public anxiety to be relieved, questions which I must say I have a lot of sympathy. I realise that more time is needed to consider the possible diversions of the service but we are under this persistent and increasing pressure to make a statement'.

An early draft of this letter said: 'I am particularly concerned about this case'. But this seems to have been left out of the final version sent to Dr Beeching. But it is indicative of the frustration felt in the transport ministry.

SAVE

THE BROAD STREET LINE!

Gospel Oak—Hampstead Heath—Finchley Road
—West End Lane—Brondesbury—Kensal Rise—
Willesden—Acton—Gunnersbury—Kew Gardens
—Richmond — Dalston — Canonbury — Highbury
and Islington—Caledonian Road—Camden Road

The line serving these areas is to be closed to passengers

If Dr. BEECHING Has His Way

Many thousands of people who travel on the line will suffer

EXTRA COST—LONGER JOURNEYS—HARDSHIP

We appeal to you — Don't let this happen—

Come and Join us at

A Mass Lobby

at the

House of Commons

on

Wednesday, May 13, at 6.30 p.m.

Issued by—The Broad Street/Richmond Line Joint Committee, 19 Burghley Road, E.11 and printed by Hillary Press (T.U.), Pollard Road, N.W.9

A week later, Margetts briefed Tom Fraser on the BRB's thinking, a 10 February minute from Scott-Maldon records the meeting, confirming that the board really wanted to shut Broad Street and sell off the site for property development: 'The great attraction from the point of view of the railways is that, in addition to producing operating economies, the changes would enable the whole of the extremely valuable Broad Street site to be thrown up for disposal'. Exactly as the Hampstead committee suspected.

It is now clear what Beeching was referring to in his letter to Anthony Royle when he said: 'This is a much more complicated question than the average passenger train withdrawal proposal'.

What is not clear is whether the possibility of a lucrative property deal was why the line was marked for closure in the Beeching reshaping report or whether it was discovered during the detailed investigations. What is certain is that, at some point, they came across the potential pot of gold which, if not at the end of the rainbow, was certainly at the end of the North London Line, and the existence of this drove all their thinking from that point onwards.[5]

At the Ministry, meanwhile, frustration with the BRB's approach continued. On 16 February – a few days after another parliamentary question – Tom Fraser talked again to Margetts who 'undertook to see what he could do to take the heat out of the protestations'.

Another minute – from Baxter to Scott-Malden – said: 'It is difficult to see what would be lost by a frank and honest statement by the board. Procrastination is causing the relationship between the public and the board to deteriorate further and the impact is felt by the minister who is having to stall on question after question'.

Meanwhile, the service cuts continued. In October 1964, BR announced Sunday closures for Canonbury, Caledonian Road, Kentish Town West and South Acton stations. It didn't need to get any ministerial approval to do this, and despite a Joint Committee census suggesting that 1,800 passengers used the four stations on Sunday, the cutback was implemented in March 1965. It allowed a cut in staff costs (Sunday working was paid at time and a half) and a slight speeding up of the service – unless you happened to live near one of these stations of course.

Under pressure from Whitehall, the pace at BR was stepped up. By May, the thinking was finally coming together; a draft position paper was circulated within the LMR for submission and approval by the British Railways Board.

---

5   There is one tantalising hint that something was in the air from the summer of 1963 however. A minute from J K Abson, in the BR estate and rating department, to F G Holt at British Transport Hotels, dated 19 July 1963, noted, while referring to the closure of the refreshment room at Broad Street: 'With the declining business at Broad Street station and *the redevelopment of the property being considered*' (Author's italics).

The old Caledonian Road station, 1960.

It said that an 'urgent decision on future policy was required' adding that continued delay would open British Railways to complaints that it was attempting to drive traffic away from the line through uncertainty and then use that as more ammunition for the closure cases – the 'closure by stealth' approach. The memo listed four options and it is clear that the possibilities of property sales at Broad Street were the driving consideration with the interests of passengers taking a back seat. The options were as follows:

Option one

Shut Broad Street station by diverting the North London Line trains to St Pancras. The Eastern's Region's suburban services, which used the Canonbury Curve to get to the North London Line and Broad Street would then be diverted too. Option one proposed to send them via King's Cross suburban, and then over the Widened Lines, the pair of tracks which parallel the Underground's Circle Line tracks from King's Cross to Moorgate.[6]

To make this possible, North London trains would leave the line east of Camden Road and then descend the single track 1-in-58 North London Incline to the level of the Midland main line and then continue to St Pancras. The incline was only used by freight traffic and its steepness and curvature meant that there was a 5mph speed limit in force.

The incline would need to be upgraded to handle passenger traffic and electrified at the DC voltage into St Pancras. Engineering opinion suggested that these were not insurmountable obstacles and the LMR Midland division confirmed that St Pancras had only limited suburban traffic and there seemed ample capacity to handle the North London Line trains if required. The cost of the improvements to the incline and DC electrification to St Pancras were estimated at £500,000.

The line east of this point would be closed to passengers, and the stations at Caledonian Road, Highbury, Canonbury, Dalston Junction and Broad Street would shut.

The position paper estimated that option one would increase the line deficit by £67,000 and there would be lost revenue of £160,000 as all passenger traffic east of Camden Road would be lost, and possibly some of that originating west of there too. This would be offset by savings of £93,000.

The crucial input came from the BR estates department – forerunner of the British Rail Property Board. It had been deeply involved in the internal discussions, and its estimate of the value of the Broad Street site if it could be sold off for development was £2.25 million – or £38.4 million in today's money.

---

6   These are the tracks which are now used by Thameslink trains between King's Cross and Farringdon.

Option two

Terminate the service at Dalston Junction, allowing the line south to Broad Street to shut, so generating the £2.25 million windfall. This option was regarded as 'commercially unsound' as Dalston was an illogical site for a passenger terminus, and any City bound passengers would have to continue their journey by bus. It was thought unlikely that they would actually bother to do this, meaning that traffic would actually be lost to rail, and so the lost revenue might offset savings. Enquiries were made of London Transport, but on 26 March 1965 LT wrote back to David Bowick, Bill Johnson's deputy at Euston, stating that buses could not handle onward traffic to the City if the North London Line stopped at Dalston and that extra buses would therefore be needed. Including this option may have stemmed from a memo from the LMR's commercial research office to the London planning committee. This contained a detailed analysis of passenger flows and came up with the surprising fact that only 35 per cent of Broad Street passengers travelled west of Dalston Junction and only 20 per cent travelled west of Canonbury.

These findings confirmed the independent research of the Hampstead Committee, and the commercial research office concluded that 'the service is not of a typical suburban character but demonstrates a patchwork of short intermediate flows somewhat similar to a bus service'.

Option three

Ignore the opposition from passengers and the growing irritation in Whitehall and press on with the closure proposal. However this was glumly dismissed on the grounds that it was 'not practical politics *at the present time*' (author's italics). The LMR thought that 'the present attitude of the minister makes it almost certain that the closure submission would not go beyond the sifting stage.'

Option four

Make the best of things, continue the service to Broad Street but achieve as many operating economies as possible. Option four contained several components

- Instead of the entire and underused terminus at Broad Street, only one island platform providing two tracks would be kept on the eastern (Liverpool Street) side of the station so providing 'minimum facilities'.
- The Eastern Region trains would still be diverted over the Widened Lines to Moorgate.
- The other stations on the line would be reduced and upgraded. 'Many of the station buildings are unnecessarily large and in an extremely poor state of repair after many years' neglect.' However, in view of what was to happen with the smaller stations it is important to note that smaller stations with fewer facilities were intended to 'help attract passengers by emphasising that we intend to offer an attractive and modern service'.

- Automated ticket issuing machines would reduce the need for staff, and would generate operational savings of £12,000 a year.
- The estates department thought that the value of the rest of the site, with a minimal presence retained, would still be £1.8 million.
- Option four would generate a total of £65,000 of savings, a figure updated after some internal discussion to £69,000.

Earlier drafts of this paper suggested that the line south from Dalston be retained, but should terminate at a new station some distance north at Worship Street. This would allow the Broad Street site to be sold while retaining a service to the City. However it would mean an inconvenient walk for passengers.

The LMR's assessment of these options was that options one and two would 'do nothing to improve the economics of the service but would enable the valuable passenger station site to be developed'. Option three was thought to be a non-starter thanks to the pressure that passengers had exerted on the ministry. So that left option four.

In June, the BRB met to accept the inevitable and to confirm that no closure proposal would be submitted. An apologetic and wordy letter to the minister explained the board's position: 'All along, this matter has been pursued by the board on the basis to ascertain whether the service could be run at a cheaper cost and means could be found of benefiting from the substantial capital appreciation in the event of it being found possible to adjust the working in a manner which would lead to releases of the maximum amount of space at Broad Street'.

All this was omitted from the official statement however, which was drafted by Johnson, Margetts and Scott-Malden, and which merely referred to BR's commitment to providing facilities to prevent travel congestion. It completely concealed the fact that a lucrative property deal at Broad Street had been uppermost in BR thinking for some time with passengers' interests coming well behind. A relieved Tom Fraser wrote to Stanley Raymond, who had succeeded Dr Beeching as chairman of the BRB, saying: 'I am very pleased, as no doubt you are, that this troublesome matter is settled'.

The reprieve was an astonishing victory for the travelling public who managed to win very few battles against British Railways in this era. The files in the National Archives make it 100 per cent certain that the endless pressure on ministers, continued questions in the House, the piles of letters to answer, media interest and three adjournment debates had made the difference, and even BR knew by spring 1965 that if it did pursue closure it would be rejected. The great investigative journalist Paul Foot, then writing for the *Sunday Telegraph*, wrote that the campaign to save the line had been run by a 'streamlined and highly organised pressure group' which was 'the most impressive of all the campaigns to save threatened lines'.[7]

---

7   *Sunday Telegraph*, 27 August 1965.

The local and joint committees then wound themselves up, a meeting to continue the committee as a rail users' group failing, attracting just three people. Probably there seemed no point in continuing once the objective had been achieved.

Despite the victory, achieved after two years of solid campaigning, Dorothy Lawrence of the Hampstead committee was surprisingly gloomy: 'There is a real danger that the service on the line will be gradually allowed to deteriorate and in a year or so there will be another proposal to close it,' she warned.

Why did the campaign succeed when so many failed? Five reasons are:

- The sheer energy and determination of the key figures themselves – maintaining a campaign over this period is an exhausting and often thankless business when facing a determined and bureaucratic adversary such as BR. The lesson was learned: well organised passenger pressure was to save the line again in the 1970s and potential opposition was a factor always taken into account when planning for the line as a result.
- The fact that this was a proposed closure in London – it affected a lot of people in a small and concentrated area where car ownership was low and buses failed to cater for this cross-town traffic. All this made it easier to mobilise opposition.
- In turn, 14 parliamentary constituencies were affected with MPs from both main parties involved.
- The campaigners had substantial material backing – finance, printing, use of halls – from the local authorities on the route.
- British Railways' own mismanagement helped the opponent's case. Although campaigners slammed 'the anti-social lunacy' of trying to run a railway on a strict profit and loss basis, they didn't need to focus solely on the difficult, political arguments over the extent to which pubic transport should be run as a publicly subsidised operation. It was reasonably easy to argue that the line would be profitable if it were run and managed and publicised properly.

It is now time to look at how British Railways went about managing the line after conceding the fight on closure.

1965–1968:
'ABSOLUTE MINIMAL FACILITIES'

In which we look at what BR did to cut costs after the line was saved, plus we take a diversion along freight lines old and new.

Having bitten the doubtless unpleasant tasting bullet, the railways started to plan for the required economies. On 22 June 1965, H C 'Bill' Johnson – who would shortly succeed Sir Stanley Raymond as chairman of the BRB – demanded of his executives:

- Do we advertise the service in a proper manner?
- Have we a fares policy to encourage traffic – especially during the off-peak?
- What was the situation regarding stations? He acknowledged that reports reaching him suggested that some were 'pretty terrible'.

His memo concluded: 'In short – we are now holding the baby – let us make it thrive'. This comment is instructive. There was to be no closure by stealth plan as feared by Dorothy Lawrence: BR really did intend to manage the service in a cheaper and more efficient manner.

The following day, Leslie Leppington, divisional manager at Euston, followed up his boss's memo by saying that illuminated signs outside stations are essential, adding that the object is to reduce facilities to the absolute minimum and to bring to a satisfactory standard the facilities which remain.

He said that handy pocket timetable cards should be produced and widely distributed and added that he expected a sympathetic hearing from local authorities when it came to planning permission for illuminated signs and changes to stations in view of the authorities vociferous opposition to closure.

All seemed to be going well. The line wouldn't be closed but managed on a more economic basis, and in the meantime the LMR would still try for a cut-down property development at Broad Street.

It proved easier said than done. Inter-regional rivalries inherited directly from pre-nationalisation days were strong, and the Eastern Region was to spoil the party. It is unclear from the files at Kew to what extent – if at all – it had been consulted over the LMR's plans for Broad Street, all of which involved the Eastern Region having to make its own arrangements for its peak hour Broad Street trains.

But on 22 July, it told its LMR colleagues that 2,100 people a day used these trains and the figure was actually rising because, in October 1964, the Underground's Moorgate to Finsbury Park branch (the ex-Great Northern and City tube) had been cut back at Drayton Park to permit work on the new Victoria Line. As a result passengers were transferring to the more convenient Broad Street trains.

Lost in the cityscape – the inconspicuous entrance to the rebuilt Finchley Road & Frognal.

Canonbury, Hampstead Heath, Finchley Road and Kensal Rise. On the Watford DC line, South Hampstead got the same treatment. The 1960s, of course, as users of London Euston and Birmingham New Street will testify, were not a good era for railway architecture.

At street level, the old wooden buildings were completely knocked down and replaced with a small white painted brick structure featuring an open entrance, a small amount of space to the right upon entering, and on the left the ticket office and staff accommodation. The person on duty would issue and collect tickets from behind this window as well as controlling access to the platforms. They gave the distinct and – correct – impression that not a single unnecessary penny had been spent, and were completely out of place with the Victorian cityscape. That at Canonbury was particularly hideous as the old stationmaster's house, in the original architecture, has remained in private occupation and looks smugly down at its replacement.

At platform levels, all the old buildings were demolished and were replaced, not by a better option, but by the cheapest option – a metal and glass bus stop shelter. In most cases, all covered access to the platforms was removed. The long platforms were reduced in length by placing a fence across halfway along and allowing the area beyond it to decay – and passengers waited miserably in the cold and the rain, the bus shelter cabins offering little protection from the elements, especially when the local vandals had smashed all the glass.

Poor maintenance on these stations meant that station lights were frequently out of commission and an early portend of the future came on 18 April 1971, when the wooden platform buildings at Kentish Town West station were completely burned down. This was probably one of a spate of arson attacks on unmanned stations in inner London which was remarkably little noticed at the time. No-one was ever caught and the station remained shut for ten years.

The bus service idiom appeared in the 1965 internal discussions on the future of the line and we have seen that North London Line passengers were using the trains more like a bus service, offering a quick and easy journey over short distances. But the idiom was completely misplaced and out of touch with passengers' instinctive views about what a railway (or above ground tube station) should look like and feel like to use. There is a world of difference between waiting five minutes for a bus on a busy high street, with shop doorways to dodge into to escape the rain, and a vandalised bus shelter on a windswept platform on a dark night with a 20-minute wait ahead of you.

The station economies only served to emphasise the gap between the tube services, offering mostly well maintained stations and a frequent and reliable service, and the inferior offering from British Railways in the capital.

At Caledonian Road the original station had a ticket office on Roman Way. The decision was taken to demolish this and construct a new entrance on Caledonian Road itself. This was a good idea, but as the platforms were orientated towards the old Roman Way entrance, the rebuild meant that passengers had to walk up a narrow and badly lit passage between the railway embankment and a retaining wall to reach platforms overlooked by the huge bulk of Pentonville prison. By night, using the station was a sinister experience that people tended not to want more than once.

South Acton partially avoided being a victim of the public convenience approach to railway station architecture. One side retained its building and canopies, although that didn't prevent local MP George Young (Conservative) complaining in 1974 that it 'looked like a building Wells Fargo would have rejected 150 years ago'. Brondesbury Park and West End Lane kept their street level buildings although the platform buildings were knocked down and bus shelters installed in their place.

Highbury & Islington was a special case. Here, until 1967, there were two stations, the huge Victorian North London Line building on the west side of Holloway Road, and the station for the Finsbury Park to Moorgate tube on the east side. Changing between them meant crossing a busy road, not that there would have been much interchange traffic to worry about at the time.

For the new Victoria line, which provided a direct link to the West End, it was decided to knock down the old North London Line station and build a brand new interchange station, with lifts being replaced by escalators for the tube trains.

This combined station was a step forward – it represented the first attempt to integrate the North London Line into the general structure of London Transport. However, the new structure was modest indeed, with no attempt to make the bold statements Charles Holden did so successfully in the 1930s. The new single-storey entrance hall was stuck unobtrusively in a courtyard behind a new Post Office, whose temporary looking 1960s building still stands today. It was an unexpected piece of modesty for a brand new station at an important road junction serving the first new tube line in London for over 50 years.

At platform level, the canopies installed when the station was rebuilt in the 1950s were retained, although the platform offices on the westbound side were shut down. The station was built and manned by London Transport and so any architectural and design strictures cannot be laid at the door of British Rail. But the station really was awkwardly designed. The tube platforms were below the east side of the main road, and so the trek up from the Victoria platforms to the North London Line was tedious and wearisome, especially as it meant going down another flight of stairs to the North London platforms once the traveller had reached ticket office level.

Some stations were luckier and escaped the architectural vandalism. Acton Central continues to resemble a well-kept Victorian railway station. At Camden Road, the main building survived intact, as did the canopied platform on the westbound side. But on the eastbound side, the buildings were demolished and a nasty brick shelter produced, giving the station a most odd appearance. At street level, the building features a coffered ceiling with cast-iron columns, the original staircases with cast-iron balustrades and wooden hand rails, leading up to the two remaining platforms. The original mid-Victorian tiled floor was carefully retained and refurbished in 1984. The station still has its outside lettering for 'Camden Town – North London Railway' and the building was partially restored and listed in 1994.

From today's perspective, the 'absolute minimal facilities' looks a cheap and nasty exercise in cost cutting. But that is an observation made with the benefit of hindsight. The LMR executives *were* fighting to cut losses, to some extent they *did* succeed, and they cannot be blamed for the breakdown in civil society which made the stations so bleak and threatening in the 1990s. Neither can they be blamed for the fact that the 1960s were a poor time both for railway design or for lacking an intelligent appreciation of the role design and architecture play in creating a pleasant public space. Indeed, local opinion regarded the new look as progress; when the old Caledonian Road station was finally knocked down, the local newspaper wrote: 'There's a glimmer of light along the line'.[12]

Returning to Holden's epochal designs for a moment, they remain at their most spectacular at night, when the intelligent use of lighting made the stations a beacon in suburbia, conveying the deliberate impression that this was a modern, safe and secure mode of travel. Eighty years on, the night-time vista available to the traveller at Oakwood, Sudbury Town or Arnos Grove retains its instructive power about intelligent use of public space.[13] The brick boxes at street level – and the desolate, badly-lit platform below – on the smaller North London Line stations provided exactly the opposite impression.

Cuts in staffing in the 1980s onwards made things even worse. Graffiti spread unchecked and women in particular began to refuse to use the services and stations after dark, especially as train reliability worsened in the 1990s. It didn't matter whether they actually were unsafe – the point was that they felt that way, the platforms felt a long way from any kind of help in emergency and

---

12   *Islington Gazette*, 8 December 1966.
13   The story of these remarkable buildings appears in Lawrence, David: *Bright Underground Spaces: The Railway Stations of Charles Holden* (Capital Transport, 2008).

the turnover of passengers on a 20-minute interval service – with poor reliability – didn't provide the reassurance that the travelling public demanded. It was all very different from the time Canonbury was noted for the well-kept garden on its platform. It is arguable indeed that this kind of minimal station infrastructure, which had 'cheap' stamped all through it like a stick of Blackpool rock, actually cost money in the medium term as the feeling of insecurity meant passengers deserted the service in droves.

A vicious circle then developed, with the railway management, confronted by falling revenues, seeking to cut costs further by reducing staffing and reducing the frequency of the service.

Meanwhile it is time to look at what Dr Beeching's plans meant for the intensive freight traffic on the North London Line. Although Beeching will always be remembered as the hammer of the rural branch line, it is less well remembered that he was no less stern with the state of British Railways' freight operations, and his assertions here were not only correct but in many ways ahead of their time.

Beeching made the fundamental point that the railways had not evolved and were still trying to compete in areas where motor transport had removed their competitive advantage. Much of BR's freight still depended on the traditional network of goods depots which generated a flow of wagons to nearby marshalling yards where they were shunted and made up in to larger trains for onward transit to other parts of the country. This traffic required a huge wagon fleet to service, meant considerable delays for the end customer, and implied wagons were rarely fully loaded. It was an unprofitable business already in decline.

The future, Beeching said, lay in a modern liner trains running point to point carrying containers which would be filled at the destination, so allowing the railways to play to their strength – the ability to transfer large loads quickly and efficiently over long distances.

The North London Line had always been a huge freight carrier, the line from Broad Street to Camden Road was four tracked, with the passenger service using the southern – electrified – pair of tracks, and goods services using the northerly pair. East of Dalston Junction the track was double rather than four tracked, but as there was no passenger service, freight again had a monopoly.

There were several sources of goods traffic over the line. The first was traffic from the former Great Eastern line using the connection from Stratford to Victoria Park. In 1953 there were 65 trains going west through Dalston each day. Many originated from the huge marshalling yard at Temple Mills, but there were also 12 trains from the Royal Group of Docks and another three from Thames Wharf, plus 11 from the Poplar and Millwall Docks. Most of these trains consisted of long rakes of covered wagons which were moved across the North London Line to marshalling yards elsewhere, where they were made up into trains for further shipment.

This dock traffic was a particular headache for operational staff as ship arrivals were unpredictable due to weather and tides. Considerable skill was needed by the traffic controllers who would need to insert a special train at short notice into an overcrowded schedule while signalling and communications were still entirely mechanical.

The line was in any case a difficult one to work into the early 1960s as steam-hauled freight traffic, often with engines in poor mechanical condition, had to be carefully squeezed in between the 20-minute electric service. There were no crossing places, and so a freight train coming off the Tottenham & Hampstead Joint line from Barking at Gospel Oak and bound for Feltham Yard on the Southern Region had no escape route until it left the North London Line at South Acton. If it broke down, delays to passenger trains would be inevitable.

The final source of traffic originated from the multitude of small goods depots which dotted the line, generating traffic of the unprofitable kind which so irritated Dr Beeching.

By the time of his report, this traffic was already in sharp decline. Road transport was just so much more convenient. Coal traffic for domestic use was also beginning to decline as solid fuels began to be phased out. Beeching wanted this traffic to be concentrated on large depots, a proposal he admitted might not find favour among smaller merchants, but in due course, they closed too as burning solid fuel in urban homes passed into history, encouraged by the Clean Air Acts.

The closures began soon after, in a piecemeal fashion. The Devons Road depot in Bow was the first to go in 1964, at the same time as the huge locomotive shed closed.

In 1965 the curious Hammersmith and Chiswick branch, which curved in a mile-long south-eastward arc away from South Acton and included two level crossings and a 15mph speed limit, finally shut. It only survived as long as it did because it served a large coal depot.

At the time of closure, receipts stood at £2,367 a year, but there was reckoned to be a benefit to net revenue of £1,904 once track and signalling were included in the sums. Hammersmith depot itself still handled a little coal traffic, but of the two private sidings, Eastman's Dye works was converting to oil, and Parry's Wharf had gone into liquidation.

A typewritten memo of a site meeting on 22 May 1965, just after closure, survives and provides a melancholy glimpse of the process of cleaning up after a freight closure. There were nine people there, representing all major departments. It was recorded that the district engineer was to recover the crossing gates over Bath Road, as well as two gas standard lamps and a Courtier stove. Two external notice boards were to be removed by the goods agent at Kew Bridge North, while the fate of one 'Safe, Milner' was to be left to the revenue accountant at Camden Depot.

Hackney Graham Road depot shut the same year; Finchley Road, Old Ford, and Hackney Wick following in 1967. Shoreditch Dunloe Street went in 1968, and on 1 July that year, Poplar Dock North (ex LNWR) and Poplar Dock South (ex GNR) also closed. Then, in March 1969, as we have seen, the Broad Street and Worship Street depots shut. Highbury & Caledonian Road closed the same year while the Kingsland Coal Depot at Dalston managed to linger on to 1972.

However, overall, the railway freight business was in transition – not decline. Beeching had been right to point to the potential of liner trains handling containers as being the way forward.

In 1965, Freightliner was born – 'Large capacity containers, specially-designed wagons and new transfer equipment provide low cost, express freight train services between exclusive road-rail terminals. It combines the advantages of rail trunk movement over medium to long distances with the flexibility of road transport for door-to-door distribution' – gushed BR's internal guide.[14]

The liner trains were a prestige project and, in June 1964, the North London's Maiden Lane depot was chosen as the first Freightliner terminal in the capital. A scale model of the new facility was carefully produced for publicity purposes, Stanley Raymond and Fred Margetts visited the 12-acre site personally, while Lance Ibbotson, chief operating officer, asked BR's director of industrial design to ensure that every single feature of the new terminal had 'the new look', adding that the impression should be one of resurgence. The terminal was renamed 'York Way' as part of the branding exercise and service began – newly electrified from the junction with the West Coast Main Line at Camden – on 7 November 1966.

Freightliner trains were normally made up of 15 flat bogie wagons loaded with containers; they were continuously coupled and ran to a strict timetable over selected routes. They carried any combination of 10ft, 20ft or 27ft (and later 30ft) containers, and so there was no waste capacity. Freightliner was a huge success – and was a real first for British Rail, and by 1971 it had broken even.

But it was too successful for the cramped York Way site and, by February 1971, Freightliner was planning to close it. Some £335,000 had been invested there, and the site employed 124 workers, but new – and highly profitable – 20-wagon container trains couldn't be operated satisfactorily there. Most customer demand was in the east and west of London and experience had shown that there was 'no need for a major terminal in London itself'.

The cramped site meant that costs per container were £2.84 at York Way, but only £1.85 at Willesden and £2.01 at Stratford. Retaining York Way would mean having to spend £7,300, mainly on providing security barriers and repairing roadways.

The closure proposal said that the 'facilities provided were very much of an experimental and interim nature'. In any case, by 1971 the fall off in industrial

---

14   *British Rail – Freightliner* publicity brochure, 1965.

and manufacturing employment in inner London was beginning to be felt. Traffic ceased in July 1971, and was shifted to Willesden and Stratford, where far more space was available. The York Way site was subsequently sold to Camden Council for housing.

But the closure of York Way did not hurt Freightliner. Container traffic from the Tilbury docks continued to use the North London Line on its way to the Midlands and North and this was joined by traffic from the vast container port at Felixstowe. The volume of this, warned British Rail executives, was such as to limit the potential for increased passenger usage – a refrain which would haunt campaigners demanding a more frequent service for decades to come.

By the time of Beeching, freight from the docks had started the rapid decline from which it never recovered, and this is perhaps a convenient time to consider the last years of the freight-only Poplar branch.

The big picture was that the new containerisation practices hit the upstream London docks very badly. Containerisation was not just vastly cheaper and quicker; it favoured ports with a large ground area and good road access, which were able to handle ships of ever-greater size. The Royal Group of Docks, even today the largest sheet of enclosed water in the world, which funnelled traffic on to the North London via Stratford, may be taken as typical. In 1977, they were handling only a third of the tonnage they were in 1970. Only ten berths remained operational – handling just two per cent of the total tonnage in the Port of London.

Faced with the decline in docks traffic, in 1967 BR simplified the horrendously complicated track layout at Poplar, the result of unplanned competition in the Victorian era. Instead of a reversal at Harrow Lane sidings and then a steep climb over the Fenchurch Street to Blackwall line to reach Poplar Dock, part of the line was re-laid on the level over the bed of the old Blackwall line.[15] The base at Poplar was reopened on 4 May 1970, with the two old depots there combined, and used only for import/export traffic.

Freight into Poplar Dock was still reasonable at the dawn of the 1970s. BR reckoned on annual receipts of £760,000, which generated a useful cash flow. But the Port of London Authority had been pressing BR to close the operation. In summer 1968 it shut Blackwall Lock as part of its rationalisation programme in the West India and Millwall Docks complex.

This was the most direct entrance to Poplar Dock, and BR believed it had a legal right of way to use it. Barges now had to use the South Lock and travel via West India Docks, a more time consuming and expensive route. The PLA promised to provide BR with equivalent rail facilities in the Royal Docks; but it felt that if BR wanted to stay at Poplar, then BR should contribute towards the cost of replacement works at Blackwall Lock.

---

15   Greater London Industrial Archaeology Society Newsletter 62, June 1979.

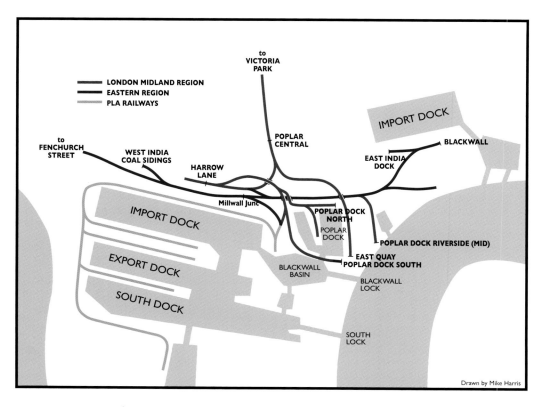

Drawn by Mike Harris

BR was not keen to move. David Bowick's analysis was that: 'We lose money on an allocated cost basis but we should be worse off by about £300,000 a year if we got out of it'. BR only paid £2,000 a year rent to the PLA while the freehold value of the site was estimated – even at depressed 1971 prices – at £650,000. Ian Campbell, the Eastern Region's general manager said, 'Certainly in the longer term we do not wish to remain in business at Poplar Dock. Nevertheless in the short term we are making more money than we could save immediately by withdrawal.'

BR really wanted to be bought out, but the matter was eventually subsumed into a Travers Morgan report into Docklands redevelopment[16] which assumed that BR would be gone by 1983. Freight, mainly to and from Thames barges, continued in the 1970s but at a fast declining rate. The end came when the Thatcher government set up the London Docklands Development Corporation to kickstart the stalled regeneration process in Docklands. This was given vast compulsory purchase powers over derelict and unused public land. By then, traffic had fallen to the point where, by the end of the 1970s, there was only 'very occasional operational use' in BR's own words, and the track south of Victoria Park had been singled in 1979.

---

16   Travers Morgan, *Docklands: Redevelopment proposals for East London*, January 1973.

So BR was happy to sell the site to the LDDC south of the proposed new Northern Docklands Relief Road (what became the A1261 Limehouse Link and Aspen Way). But it wanted to keep a presence north of this road in the hope of winning freight business from the vast redevelopments planned at what became Canary Wharf.

The sale of Poplar Dock was then held up by a dispute with the PLA over restrictive covenants in BR's lease, which dated from 1851 and insisted upon continued railway use, something which could have hit the value of the site. These issues were eventually solved and the site closed on 2 October 1981. Development was slow in the recession hit 1980s, and the classic British Railways enamel goods yard signs, generally unloved by railwayana collectors because of their huge size, stood forlornly by locked exit gates at Poplar Dock North for years after all rail activity had ceased.

BR never got any freight traffic from the huge construction sites at Canary Wharf – a far greater need was to provide transport for workers expected to move to there, and in 1983 a bill went before Parliament for the second stage of the Docklands Light Railway. This would use the trackbed from Poplar to the GER main line into Stratford and services here started in 1985.

No thought at all seems to have been given to retaining the line and running North London Line trains over the branch to serve Canary Wharf.

Public convenience style architecture: Canonbury station.

1968–1985: 'FINANCIAL ANARCHY'

In which we look at how Harold Wilson's government grappled with the post Beeching world; how the North London Line survived yet another threat, watch as a new protest group is formed, and study how the Greater London Council stepped in to support the line.

In 1966 and 1967 two transport White Papers[17] finally made an attempt to deal with the legacy of Beeching. The 1967 White Paper on rail policy said that the requirement in the 1962 Act for BRB to pay its way by the beginning of 1968 was 'entirely unrealistic' and would, if pursued, force it into actions which would be against the interests of the community. It acknowledged that there were many lines which had 'little or no prospect of paying their way, yet whose value to the community outweighs their accounting cost'. Crucially, these lines included many urban commuter services, whose closure would 'add intolerably to road congestion' as well as rural and cross-country services.

The Transport Act which followed in 1968 allowed the government to pay BR a formal subsidy – known as Grant Aid – where (a) a line lost money, (b) it was socially or economically desirable for the services to continue, and (c) it was financially unreasonable to expect BR to provide those services without a grant. This Act was a big a step forward for UK transport policy. It acknowledged for the first time that railways fulfilled a social function, and that this function was part of their core activities, and it implied too that there should be no more mass closures.[18] The 1969 BRB annual report said that the railways themselves were glad to be free of the 'odium of seeking to withdraw a passenger service where the loss of social benefit clearly exceeds the savings to the railway'. (Bill Johnson and Fred Margetts had both sat on the joint steering committee which worked on the 1967 White Paper.)

The fate of the North London Line was intimately tied up with the Euston to Watford DC service, and together they were among the very first Grant Aid requests submitted by the LMR. The latter was one of the highest loss makers in the region, with a deficit in 1965/66 of £479,000. Part of the loss stemmed from the commercial deal with London Transport to run Bakerloo Line trains on to Watford. BR kept all the revenue but paid all the operating costs so if the service was uneconomic, BR took the hit – not London Transport. As BR struggled to contain its losses, the Bakerloo trains (which ran every 20 minutes throughout the day in 1963) were cut back at Queen's Park in June 1965 so that only a handful ran from Watford at peak times.

---

17   *Transport Policy 1966*, Cmd 3057 and *Rail Policy 1967*, Cmd 3439.
18   Some significant closures did continue however, including the Carlisle to Edinburgh Waverley route in 1969 and, scandalously in 1970, the ending of the electric expresses on the Woodhead route between Sheffield and Manchester which did not even appear in the Beeching report's closure list.

Homeward bound – Broad Street in the 1970s.

By the close of 1965, the LMR was considering axing the Euston and Broad Street local services to Watford completely, but in the end, it did not have the appetite for another political fight over public transport cuts in north-west London. Instead, with plans to cut the annual loss to £200,000, partly by restricting Bakerloo Line trains, the LMR recommended to the BRB that the service be retained.

There seemed little point either in retaining the Watford DC service and axing that to Broad Street, even though this was a service in long-term decline. In 1963 it was losing £46,000 a year, and patronage was falling quickly. In 1962, there were 42,000 passenger miles, falling to 37,000 in 1964, 32,000 in 1966, and just 28,000 in 1967. A 24 November 1966 memo to the LMR's planning managers said the traffic from north of Bushey and Oxhey was 'killed with electrification' and most passengers used the new high-speed AC service via Euston. It added: 'The normal Broad Street – Watford service is hardly attractive; if completely untouched it will continue to decline; if completely withdrawn, apart from the problem of peak hour loading north of Queen's Park, there will be difficulties in providing reasonable capacity on the North London Line'.

But in return for Grant Aid it was agreed to cut the service frequency from 15 to 20 minutes for both the Euston trains and the peak hour service into Broad Street. The Saturday morning Broad Street to Willesden Low Level trains were withdrawn from 12 November 1966.

The LMR also told the transport ministry the facts of life on urban transport – increasing revenue on these lines was simply not possible; each successive fare increase, it reported, had been followed by a progressive reduction in the number of passengers, and hence, of revenue.

In due course the transport ministry agreed Grant Aid for the LMR DC network as follows:
- 1969: Broad Street – Richmond £439,000, and Euston/Broad Street – Watford £523,000
- 1970: Broad Street – Richmond £478,000 and Euston/Broad Street – Watford £497,000
- For 1971 the Grant Aid was given across the entire Region without a line by line breakdown

For a while there was, therefore, an uneasy stalemate.

Richmond – March 1969.

But at the June 1970 General Election, the Conservatives under Ted Heath were unexpectedly returned to office, and this heralded an ideologically driven return to cutting subsidies to unprofitable railways. The aim was that all subsidies would be phased out by 1973. The threat to the North London Line was alive again.

A new North London Line Committee (NLLC), sprung into life, based in Hampstead and led initially by Kay Peacock, a Liberal Party GLC candidate in 1970, and a Save the Broad Street Line Committee was formed in Richmond. Both groups stemmed out of two passenger meetings that the LMR had attended at Gospel Oak and Kew Gardens in the summer of 1971.

At the Gospel Oak meeting, Brian Rusbridge, the LMR's London divisional manager, told the 100-strong audience that passenger costs in 1970 were £789 million, compared with revenue of £311 million, although freight traffic was profitable. He agreed that a rise in fares would not be the solution: 'If I doubled the fares tomorrow we would still only reach break-even point and the public can only stand so much'. London commuters had already been hit with a swingeing – up to 25 per cent – fare increase in March 1971, designed to reduce the government subsidy by £11 million.[19]

The NLLC's dynamic was subtly different from the original committee which had to stave off a direct threat to the line and which viewed British Railways as being in some sense the enemy. The new committees worked hard to build friendly relations with BR managers, sympathising with the impossible position they were placed in by the government's short-termism. Kay Peacock said it was, 'Quite unreasonable to expect British Rail's management to operate on this hand to mouth basis'.

The NLLC never had more than 12–13 members at any one time, but it produced reasoned reports full of facts and figures and a good deal of intellectual rigour. Its members worked tirelessly on publicity campaigns to promote the line. It received some financial support from local councils along the line and was a highly effective pressure group which was taken seriously both by BR management and transport civil servants.

Reading archives of NLLC paperwork years later transports you back into an apparently archaic, pre-internet, pre-Facebook world of typewritten and duplicated leaflets which needed people to physically get out and distribute them and build direct human interactions. That in fact was how political campaigning worked back then and Chris Austin, a BR executive deeply involved in NLL matters, recalls that the NLLC was probably the most vocal and effective of all the passenger groups around at the time.

Just as years before, the NLLC carried out a cost/benefit analysis to prove that any savings from withdrawing the Grant Aid, which would surely lead to

19   The Tories justified the increase by saying: 'Treating the London commuter network as a single entity and aiming to make it viable as soon as possible was just as much the policy of the previous administration as it is of the present one'. *Hansard*, 11 May 1971.

closure, were a total illusion. A closure following the withdrawal of Grant Aid might save the government money, but this saving would be massively offset by the greater costs to society as a whole.

Camden Council, supported by City, Hackney, Islington, Hammersmith and Hounslow authorities, met BR executives at an emergency session on 20 December 1971 to discuss the threat. BR told them that there was no intention at present to withdraw services but warned that 'it must reserve its position' if heavy losses continued. Camden accepted that BR couldn't give the assurances it wanted and demanded a meeting with ministers. The latter refused, saying that no closure proposal had been tabled.

The uncertainty continued throughout 1972, a year which saw the publication of the NLLC's *Save the North London Line*. The committee reckoned that the real cost to the community of closing the service would actually be over £1 million a year – almost three times the cost of the Grant Aid subsidy. The calculations were as follows:

Table four – the real cost of closure

Annual revenue and expenses	£
Operating cost of passenger services	768,000
Less earnings	391,000
= total annual savings by withdrawing subsidy	377,000
Direct cost of closure	**£**
Cost to passengers of extra time needed to take bus services	751,000
Indirect cost of closure	**£**
Cost of providing and operating more buses	540,000
Less calculated revenue assuming the same fares as on rail	250,000
Total indirect costs of closure	290,000
TOTAL ANNUAL COSTS OF CLOSURE	1,041,000

Meanwhile, the threat to the entire railway system seemed to be deepening: in October that year the *Sunday Times* revealed secret government plans to slash the rail network from 11,600 miles to just 6,700 miles.

In the event, Grant Aid for the London commuter network was renewed for one year in January 1972, and again a year later.

decline. Industry was vanishing, and population was falling. All the inner London boroughs were losing population and all but one or two outer ones were doing so too.

High office rents in the centre, kept artificially high by the difficulties in getting development permits, were persuading more companies to relocate to cheaper suburban locations, or to out of London centres such as Reading, Guildford and the New Towns, which were establishing substantial employment bases of their own.

As a result, jobs in central London had fallen by 14 per cent. This managed decline was actually official policy for London as fewer people meant less demand for housing; years after the end of the Second World War, the housing shortage remained entirely unresolved. But it had the logical result that rail journeys into the centre had fallen seven per cent between 1966 and 1973. This decline was expected to continue; if the current trends were extrapolated, thought the study's authors, the 1966 to 1991 decline in rail commuting would be a staggering 90 per cent. Car ownership had risen too – London registrations were up by 50 per cent between 1963 and 1972, although 63 per cent of inner London households still didn't have a car.

This decline seemed an unpromising picture to call for more investment in London's transport. But against a background of increasingly dispersed journeys, better facilities for cross-London travel looked a good idea, and the report conceded that *Ring Rail* was 'on the face of it an attractive proposition'. But Barran still recommended against pursuing the idea because the £100 million cost claimed by *Ring Rail* would almost certainly turn out to be a very large underestimate. If it generated 2–6,000 journeys each way in the peak it would not justify the huge expense.

There was also the fact that making the system work would require more main line trains to make an extra stop short of their terminus, for example at the proposed Vale Royal interchange north of King's Cross. This would have been an operating nightmare for rail managers. Instead was the recommendation that two cheaper options should be taken forward to a feasibility study:

- A radial service from North Woolwich, extended over the freight only section of the North London Line through Hackney, and then after Willesden, joining the Great Western main line near Acton and taking in the West Ealing-Greenford loop. For a cost of £2 million it thought a diesel service using clapped out stock (not the report's actual words of course) could be provided with a 20-minute headway between trains. This might generate 2–3,000 peak hour journeys daily.
- A better bet was to spend £25 million and provide an electrified service along this route, although that would mean engineering works to Hampstead Tunnel. But it was the preferred solution as it would probably generate 50 per cent more traffic as electrification would allow trains to run every 10 minutes.

The *London Rail Study* also proposed to divert the Barking to Kentish Town diesel service over the North London Line via a new spur to Gospel Oak. This would then follow the West London Line after Willesden and terminate at Clapham Junction.

So far so good. Realistic and affordable options had been tabled. And then the Labour government vetoed the plans. Transport secretary Neil Carmichael cited insufficient track capacity and in particular the fact that slower freight trains needed two and a half times the track capacity of passenger trains when the two interwork. Hampstead Tunnel was also a problem as it is so narrow that trains cannot pass through it in opposite directions at the same time.[24] Almost certainly the real issue was money – the long crisis of the 1974 to 1979 Labour government was already underway.

However, the idea of *Ring Rail* never went away – a considerable achievement for 'the three young men working independently and without sponsorship'. And agitation for a better deal on public transport continued, especially in Hackney, where there was no tube service. The borough's residents consequently suffered a poor connection to the West End, and there were demands for the missing link to be reinstated between Dalston and Stratford.

The next crisis on the North London Line had a subtext which would become one of the key themes in UK transport in the next two decades – democratic control of public transport in the capital.

The first shot was fired on 30 June 1975, when the Labour government, which had started with a pro-rail approach, responded to the growing financial crisis by telling British Rail to cut its subsidies to loss making services, just as the Tories had done. BR immediately started to plan for swingeing service cuts and fare increases. Under the Transport (London) Act 1969, it had a duty to consult the Greater London Council, which was the strategic transport authority for the capital, on fares and services. However, what this consultation really meant had never been tested.

On 14 November, Geoff Huskisson, the LMR's London divisional manager, spelled out the cuts in detail on a line per line basis – for the North London Line this would be a reduction in service frequency from every 20 to every 30 minutes, the same on Sundays, and a frequency reduction on the Broad Street to Watford peak hour service to 30 minutes also. The North London Line Committee warned that the cuts would make the NLL 'no longer a walk on service but one where journeys had to be planned in advance'.

Faced with these cutbacks, the GLC was not entirely powerless. Under the 1969 Act, it had no control over how British Rail managed the service, but it did have the right to pay a subsidy to BR to maintain service levels. However, this power had never been used. Urgent investigations were ordered as to its feasibility on this occasion.

---

24   *Hansard*, 20 December 1974.

Dalston Junction 1981 – the buildings to the left have now been demolished.

City-bound at Finchley Road in 1984 – note the bus shelter on the platform. The graffiti above the tunnel entrance warns that it is a virtual miners' picket line.

Near Caledonian Road – the Ebonite factory tower on York Way, a prominent local landmark, was demolished in 1983.

County Hall saw the North London Line as an anomaly; it was the only true non-radial route, one which was entirely within London but where fares and services were entirely outside the control of the peoples' representatives. Services and facilities were grossly inferior to those on the tube, and had every prospect of getting worse still, while the proposals in the 1974 *London Rail Study* were, it seemed, dead in the water.

By 22 November, the GLC heard that Whitehall would neither reconsider the cuts on British Rail, nor force BR to divert the impact away from London which would be worst hit. Negotiations began, and on this basis the service cuts, scheduled for 1 January 1976, were postponed to March. On 24 February – with only a week to go – a solution was devised. The GLC would pay a subsidy of £150,000 to maintain service levels until the end of the year on the understanding that this was an emergency measure and that the cuts would be implemented if no longer term solution was agreed.

It seemed a good solution – on the surface. And crucially it was the first time a major metropolitan authority had provided cash support for train services. Yet over at BR, chairman Richard Marsh, a former Labour transport minister, was unhappy – he told the GLC in a letter of 22 February that 'we are skating on thin ice financially' adding that ad-hoc subsidies from local authorities to services already heavily subsidised through the PSO could lead to 'financial anarchy'.

Not everyone at County Hall was happy either. The feeling grew that they were being held to ransom by British Rail, which provided an inferior service entirely within the GLC area, and which didn't consult on fares and services. Even so, a similar subsidy was agreed a month later for the heavily loss-making Tottenham – Stratford – North Woolwich service, where BR had planned to scrap all off-peak trains and cut the peak hour service by half.

Almost immediately, GLC prepared to renew the deal for 1977. In the autumn the GLC offered a 1977 subsidy of £200,000 for the North London and North Woolwich services. The offer was contemptuously rejected by BR on 30 September, saying there was 'no question of bargaining over this amount' – BR wanted £300,000 or the service cuts would begin. The GLC quickly conceded, and a press statement headed 'GLC may buy off rail cuts again' seemed an accurate summary of the situation.

The GLC felt it was on more doubtful ground when it came to cuts to services which lay partly within the GLC area and partly outside. This included the Euston to Watford DC service, where the frequency – in the absence of GLC subsidies – was cut to 30 minutes from March 1976, as well as a whole set of Southern Region suburban services. BR wanted £450,000 to maintain service levels on these, and the GLC baulked at the implications of agreeing. If they conceded, they feared they would open up a principle that British Rail could hold them to ransom on service levels when they had no real control.

They decided to keep their nerve, especially as the services affected several non-London authorities, and the axe duly fell. One memo from the period complained that there had to be a long term solution to this matter to avoid the council 'being forced into a position of ill-informed, last minute, ad-hoc reactions to board proposals'.

The principle of subsidy being established for the North London Line, the GLC moved to force London Transport, which it now controlled, to include the line on the tube map. A letter of 22 April 1976 shows LT still remaining obdurate, citing the difference between their frequent services and the sub-standard services on offer on the North London Line as a reason for not including it.[25]

The battle over the tube map was one which LT was now bound to lose, as the GLC, having paid out large amounts of public money in subsidy, was determined to do everything in its power to publicise the line, which would help attract new passengers to it. The line duly appeared on the tube map in 1977. However, LT still refused to display the line with its own colour or with a bolder outline – the two factors which made the tube map so easy to understand – and it didn't appear in the 1978 edition of the map produced for use with pocket diaries.

---

25   North London saw some guerrilla action during this period, when volunteers pasted an overlay on to tube maps so that the North London Line was visible! Behind the action was Michael Ellman, lawyer, Liberal Party activist and leader of a group called Hackney Citizens Rights.

The NLLC was convinced of the centrality of good publicity – it pointed to a 12.5 per cent growth in off-peak ticket sales between summer 1976 and summer 1977, compared with only a 3.5 per cent rise the year before, and argued that some of this was due to the line appearing on the tube map. BR management seemed to share much of this thinking, but a quietly despairing letter to the NLLC from the LMR's divisional manager in August 1976 is worth quoting in full: 'It is indeed a most difficult thing to acquaint a local population of the availability of public transport in their area,' it ran, 'even though the station has been there for over a century, and some of the residents have lived adjacent for their lifetimes, our experience elsewhere only underlines the fact that people can live almost next door to a station and still not know where the trains run and the journeys which can be made'.

He went on: 'Frankly I cannot see any reasonable form of media which we have not tried, Capital Radio, local press, house to house distribution of

Industrial Willesden – a Broad Street train overlooked
by the now demolished Acton Lane power station.

leaflets, new maps, enlisting the aid of local councils, producing car stickers, beer mats, apart from more conventional means'.

The initially rocky relationship between the GLC and BR improved quite quickly as more ambitious schemes were discussed, and crucially, it survived the May 1977 elections, which saw the Conservatives under the flamboyant and bow-tied Horace Cutler regain control of the GLC. Cutler's transport spokesman, Harold Mote, had made threatening noises about the need to reduce transport subsidies, but in fact the Conservatives continued Labour's policy of working with BR to improve the North London Line. Jonathan Roberts recalled the NLLC breathing a huge sigh of relief: 'On day one we could have lost it', he says today.

In 1978, British Rail said that no contribution would be expected from the GLC to maintain service levels in recognition of the work already being put in terms of publicity. The scene was set for a fruitful partnership in the next few years.

"The future of the line is by no means certain..."
"...wide gap between costs and earnings..." BRITISH RAIL

SAVE THE BROAD ST. LINE!

PUBLIC MEETING and EXHIBITION

ISLINGTON TOWN HALL
Upper Street

TUESDAY 18TH JANUARY 8 P.M.

Speakers include:

JOHN GRANT M.P.

ALEC McGUIRE PASSENGER MANAGER BRITISH RAIL

Put your questions and point of view

admission free

NORTH LONDON LINE COMMITTEE — ISLINGTON
SECRETARY ROBIN CAVE 33 CANONBURY PARK SOUTH N1

1979–1985: 'NOT AS RELIABLE AS WE WOULD HAVE LIKED'

In which we look at how BR got on when they reopened a railway rather than closing one, in this case the missing link between Dalston and Stratford.

The railway bridge over Mare Street was a standing annoyance to the citizens of Hackney. Almost within sight of Hackney Town Hall, it carried the freight only tracks of the North London from Dalston to Stratford and the frequent trains crossing it only served to remind residents of how irritating it was that they couldn't hop on a train and switch to the Victoria Line at Highbury in order to get to the West End.

By the late 1970s, it was actually becoming something more than an annoyance. Like most of working class London, there was a tradition of people working very locally, often within walking distance, in clothing, printing, woodworking and engineering factories.

But these traditional industries were in terminal decline, the victims, usually, of years of under investment. Unemployment was rising fast, and young people in particular were hard hit; Britain's inner city crisis had begun.

And since inner cities were also areas of large ethnic minority settlement there was an extra dimension to the growing crisis; racial discrimination meant that the children of West Indian immigrants in particular found jobs especially hard to get. Complaints about police harassment were the trigger for a series of riots, most notably at the Notting Hill Carnival in 1976 and again in 1977. On the other hand the National Front, a neo-fascist political party, was picking substantial support in London's East End. At the GLC elections of 1977, which were based on Parliamentary constituency boundaries, the party picked up 10–15 per cent of the vote across large areas of north and east London, peaking at 19.4 per cent in Shoreditch. Mass opposition to this organisation led to more riots, at Lewisham and Wood Green in 1977.

Many inner city areas were, not coincidentally, often ones where public transport was poor. Hackney was not served by the tube, and while there was a good Eastern Region service to the City, the decline of walk-to-work jobs meant people in much of Hackney found it hard to compete for jobs elsewhere because of the poor public transport.

On paper, the area was served by a good bus service. In practice it wasn't like that if you needed to take two buses to get to work on time. Car ownership in inner London was still well below the national average, but it was rising and making the roads more and more congested for bus traffic. Canny employers would often use distance to work as a deciding factor when assessing job candidates. So improving public transport was a must if such areas were to be revitalised.

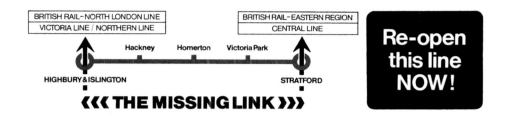

BRITISH RAIL – NORTH LONDON LINE
VICTORIA LINE / NORTHERN LINE

BRITISH RAIL – EASTERN REGION
CENTRAL LINE

Hackney   Homerton   Victoria Park

HIGHBURY & ISLINGTON   STRATFORD

‹‹‹ THE MISSING LINK ›››

Re-open this line NOW!

A pressure group – Hackney Public Transport Action Committee (HAPTAC) – had been formed as early as 1971 to fight for a better deal in the notoriously tubeless borough. It was the brainchild of Frank Billings, a leading member of the NLLC and the London Passenger Action Confederation, and it had three objectives:

- Restore trains over the freight only section of the North London Line between Dalston and Stratford.
- Campaign for the Chelsea – Hackney tube.
- Fight for improvements to the unsatisfactory bus services.

In 1973 HAPTAC wrote to BR asking for a diesel service to be restored from Stratford to Highbury via Hackney on a 15/20-minute interval basis. HAPTAC got nowhere – BR flatly refused to take the request any further, saying that it would be an unviable proposition to restore a service which had not operated for many decades, especially as its focus was on getting passengers to central London.

Billings died in 1974 and HAPTAC's leading light soon became Roger Lansdown, an economist with Hawker Siddeley who had just bought his first house in Lower Clapton. Lansdown already had community campaigning experience, having been among those who fought to save the Royal Agricultural Hall in Islington. He was later to be involved in the Save Liverpool Street Station Campaign. His neighbour in Clapton was Richard Gee, a Hackney councillor who helped get HAPTAC taken seriously by the council. There were never more than half a dozen people involved in HAPTAC at any time, but they included Hackney councillors, and as with the North London Line Committee, dedicated and focussed people working together found they could wield an influence out of all proportion to their numbers.

The growing crisis, which was intimately linked with the plans to refurbish London's collapsing Docklands, meant that there was (some) government money available for projects which would regenerate these areas. Government approved projects could be financed through Urban Aid Grants, with central government picking up 75 per cent of the bill, and the local authority concerned the remaining 25 per cent.

Fortunately, the GLC as we have seen was now developing a more activist role towards public transport. In 1973–74, 72 per cent of GLC transport spending was going on highways – by 1975–76, under the new Labour administration,

68 per cent was going on public transport.[26] A raft of transport improvement proposals duly appeared in the 1976 *London Docklands Strategic Plan* – published by a statutory joint committee made up of the GLC and the five Docklands boroughs.

The report still aspired to maintain a viable port in the capital. It listed improvements to the North Woolwich service and building an interchange with the District Line at West Ham as priority one projects, and electrification of the former line as priority three. The building of a new tube line was to be found in the priority two class, doubtless because it came with a price tag of £140–160 million attached.

A key significance of this plan was the realisation that public transport had a major part to play in urban regeneration. Another was that not everything had to be based around travel to and from central London.

The first step in executing this plan came in 1977, when the GLC agreed to pay £1.3 million towards the modernisation of the semi-derelict stations on the North Woolwich branch; this line was in dire straits, with traffic in free fall due to the collapse of the London docks and associated industry. Between 1971 and 1975 it had lost 45 per cent of its traffic and it was allegedly the worst loss maker, per capita, on all of British Rail, having lost £282,000 in 1973.

The track was singled from Custom House on to North Woolwich where a simplified new station was built, with the architecturally pleasant but very dilapidated terminus scheduled to become a museum. The stations at Silvertown, Custom House and Canning Town were all rebuilt, and a brand new interchange with the District Line was built at West Ham. All this work was completed by 1980. These turned out to be among the few achievements of the plan, which was scrapped when the Thatcher government handed control of the entire Docklands programme to the unelected London Docklands Development Commission (LDDC).

In 1978, BR chairman Sir Peter Parker finally announced that BR wanted to implement the proposals in the *London Rail Study* and bridge the missing link by providing a new service which would join the North London Line to the North Woolwich branch.

The first trains began running on 14 May 1979, so restoring a facility which had been absent since 1942. There was a Monday to Friday only diesel service from the North Woolwich branch to Stratford and over the North London Line, terminating at Camden Road. It ran every 20 minutes during the peak hours, and every 30 minutes during the rest of the day until around nine in the evening. It was operated by two-car diesel units of late 1950s vintage. It was marketed as the Crosstown link, and in July and August Newham residents were offered a flat 30p fare to any station on to the entire North London Line on presentation of a special voucher.

---

26   *The plight of Inner London and Ring Rail* – Ring Rail Group.

BR leaflet for the reopening of the Missing Link in 1979.

...Hackney Central...

Hackney Wick... Two new

stations on the Crosstown Linkline

...Open from May 1980...

CROSSTOWN
LINK
LINE

≳ British Rail

The new service was financed through the Urban Aid Grant scheme, with a total cost of £1.47 million, of which 25 per cent was paid for by the GLC. The official opening, by Sir Peter Parker of BR and Sir Horace Cutler, was not until 11 June; however, it was carried out in secrecy to avoid the possibility of it being disrupted by anti-nuclear demonstrators. Nuclear waste from the power stations at Sizewell and Bradwell passed this way on the journey to be reprocessed at Sellafield.[27]

New stations were opened at Hackney Central, on the site of the North London Railway station, and at Hackney Wick, some 300 yards away from the old Victoria Park station, on 12 May 1980. They were built with minimal facilities and offered indifferent cover from the elements both at platform level and on the walk up to them. At Hackney Central the old North London Railway street level buildings, which had gone through a varied set of uses since 1944, were not restored, and a small building suitable for one-man operation and control appeared instead. Sir Peter Parker admitted: 'Yes, they have got no loos; they're not practical things to have in a more economic station'.[28] Hackney Wick was unfortunately sited: 'In the middle of a run-down industrial estate', said one BR observer, and traffic was disappointing.

The coming of the government Urban Aid programme made grants available for qualifying community projects, and HAPTAC won enough in grants to employ a series of full time researchers. One of them was a Yorkshireman named John Sanderson, who was also to play a big part in North London Line history.

---

27   Anti-nuclear campaigners dubbed these trains the Radiation Expresses. They still run today, but there have been no incidents and concern over them seems to have subsided.

28   *Daily Telegraph*, 12 June 1979.

The new diesel service was something of a holding operation while successive governments dithered over the huge cost of extending the Jubilee Line to serve Docklands. New stations were planned at Homerton in the east of the borough, which would serve a densely populated area where a brand new hospital was being built, and at Dalston. That at Homerton couldn't be built until the line was finally electrified, as the insertion of another stop would mean the diesel services, which suffered from poor acceleration, would then lose their path amid the electrically operated trains west of Dalston.

The new Dalston station got off to a bad start. BR originally wanted to build at Ridley Road market, but reaction there was heavily against and 5,000 people signed a petition against it. The NLLC condemned what it called 'a poky station entrance down a side street' and Hackney Council refused planning consent in September 1978.

Eventually a site on the west side of Kingsland Road was chosen, on the site of the former North London Railway Kingsland station which had closed as far back as 1865 when the line to Broad Street opened. The GLC agreed to pay £12,000 for the abortive design costs in the first scheme. This was a much better building than the 1980 stations, with covered access down to the platforms, which also provided plenty of cover against the rain, together with a pleasing brick structure at street level. It suffered however from short platforms which could only support three-car trains, something not considered to be an issue at the time. It opened – named Dalston Kingsland to distinguish it from Dalston Junction on the Broad Street line – on 16 May 1983. Homerton opened on 13 May 1985.

For the curious north Londoner, eager to fully explore his city, the new service provided a fascinating glimpse of an unknown world – and one approaching the very nadir of its fortunes.

From Stratford the line passed areas of mainly low-rise housing with the skyline peppered by the occasional tower block. (Newham had 118 tower blocks – more than any other local authority.) Past Canning Town the train entered the core of London's dockland. The diesel units gave the passenger with the foresight to grab a seat behind the driver a fine all round view of the dereliction. By Custom House station the dockside cranes were just visible behind the three-storey warehouses erected in the 1950s, but the former PLA exchange sidings were derelict.

The train then dived at 1 in 50 into the Connaught Tunnel below the docks to emerge at Silvertown, which had the feel of an island community, cut off from the rest of London by the docks to the north and the Thames to the south. At Silvertown the famous Tate & Lyle sugar refinery soared above the rebuilt station. On to North Woolwich the train rattled, between Factory Road on the right and Albert Road on the left, with the river tantalisingly hidden from view by more huge factories.

Nigel Wood, a former guard on the line, recalls: 'Still using tail lamps, we guards had to call Custom House signalbox before leaving in case Silvertown Tunnel flooded, the old station, semi derelict by now, manned by Doris, the leading railwoman, from 06.00 to 18.00 like all other stations on the line. A railman would travel up on the last train at 19.35 and lock all the stations, usually having a swift pint in the Royal Pavilion pub outside the station before departure.'

But this was an area in catastrophic decline – unemployment was growing by three times the London rate. It wasn't just the docks; Tate & Lyle[29] had been shedding jobs themselves, as had Gulf Oil at Minoco Wharf. AEI Cables was just a memory; the iconic Beckton Gas Works finally shut in 1970 and in 1976, STC (Western Electric) went too, taking 2,000 more jobs with it. By the time the new diesel service opened up, industry was in full retreat along with the docks themselves, where the last ship called in 1981. Much of the industry which remained, said the LDDC, was there only because of low rents in poor quality properties and it was probably the most depressed area in the entire capital.

The pleasant, 1847 terminus at North Woolwich was derelict, and the site was overlooked by two 19-storey tower blocks of 1962 vintage: Queensland House and Westland House. It was a zone of collapsing walls and boarded up buildings, and perhaps the most powerful impression remaining from that period was the mournful silence of it all.

Meanwhile the GLC had become involved in the case of Kentish Town West station, which was still shut after the 1971 fire. Behind the scenes, the LMR had tried to close this permanently in February 1973, and had got to the point of asking for government approval to start the statutory closure procedure. (It was told to wait for the result of the London Rail Study.)

A Camden Council compulsory purchase order for land adjoining the station was the trigger for the closure proposal. Camden proposed to use this land as public open space rather than for any commercial purposes. Camden agreed with the BR Property Board that they would lift the CPO if the fate of Kentish Town West was determined.

---

29   Some 500 people still work at Tate & Lyle – the last major factory left in the old East End.

So on 1 December, 1975, BR asked the environment department civil servants for permission to invoke the statutory closure process. They got an astonishing reply from Brian Enright at the DoE. He told BR that it wasn't actually necessary to use the statutory process as the Transport Act referred to 'existing' rail services and here there was no 'existing' rail service in place to be closed. Practically speaking, he warned, launching the closure process might 'Awaken latent public pressure to reopen the station. This would be most unfortunate both for the government and the board in the present climate of restraint in public spending'.

Another note, from the chief passenger manager for social services (that is, subsidised services) to the executive director (passenger) explained that the DoE's 'worry is the local pressure group'. He meant, of course, the North London Line Committee.

To their credit, British Rail's own lawyers were having none of this devious subterfuge, ruling that if BR formally closed the station without invoking the legal procedure there could be legal challenges if it then sold the site.

On 15 April 1976, Ken Peter at the DoE told BR it could go ahead, the GLC were given the news on 27 May, and the initial section 54 notices – giving notice of the intent to withdraw service – were published on 11 June.

Camden Council immediately hit the roof. The wording of the notices gave the clear impression that Camden agreed with the closure. B H Wilson, Camden's chief executive wrote to Geoff Huskisson, the LMR divisional manager, with 'serious concern' complaining that the notices: 'Would clearly give the impression that my council are supporting the closure of the station in order to achieve the extension of the public open space. This is not the position and I can find nothing in the correspondence which indicates otherwise'.

Camden immediately issued a press release condemning BR, while internally, the LMR general manager mused that 'the divisional manager, London has no option but to apologise to the council'.

For the North London Line Committee, Jonathan Roberts complained that it was 'Very unfortunate that the good liaison arrangements which have been established between ourselves and the LMR London division of BR seem to have broken down on this occasion'. BR had in fact, failed to inform the NLLC that it was planning to go ahead with the closure.

In reply, the NLLC produced a detailed cost benefit study which argued that the reopening would be justified if it generated 500,000 passenger journeys per year. At Euston, LMR staff spent some time trying to refute this. They estimated that had it been open, the figure for passenger journeys would be a maximum of 395,000 a year 'due to the continuing fall in population of the area and BR's policy of maximising fare revenue. It just does not seem possible for traffic levels to rise significantly in the near future.' They thought that the NLLC study also didn't take into account the reduction of traffic at Gospel Oak and Camden Road if Kentish Town West reopened.

The old station at Hackney Central. This building is now a nightclub.

The cost of rebuilding in 1971 was estimated at £85,000 – by October 1976, inflation had raised this to £188,000. But on 25 November 1977, BR won government approval for the closure, even though the TUCC, which had received objections from the GLC, Camden, the NLLC and North London Polytechnic, as well as the Kentish Town West Save Our Station Committee, considered that there would be hardship for some, especially children, the elderly and the handicapped.

BR was relieved at its victory. It had been alarmed at the implications of the TUCC rejecting closure – the LMR general manager's office had noted: 'If the matter does eventually go against us then a definite question mark must obviously be set against all future closure proposals in the London area'. The TUCC conclusions were, he said, 'to say the least surprising'.

BR then agreed to suspend the formal closure while the GLC considered whether to step in. And on 18 May 1979, the GLC agreed to pay for the rebuilding based on the figures BR had provided, which now had an upper estimate of £299,000. The station was finally reopened – fully vandal proof – on 5 October 1981.

By then, a potentially important piece of the jigsaw had slotted into place. The date was 5 January 1981, when the diesel service from Barking to Kentish Town over the Tottenham & Hampstead Joint line was diverted to terminate at Gospel Oak instead. This was, in part, another *London Rail Study* recommendation, but the real impetus for the change was the electrification of the London St Pancras to Bedford service, which made it hard for the diesel units to fit into Kentish Town station.

On paper, this diversion deprived users of the service of a good connection to the Northern Line tube at Kentish Town. In practice, another cross-London service connecting with the North London at Gospel Oak would provide much better onward connections. Traffic was sparse on the western section of the line, and passengers aiming for central London were not using the Barking to Kentish Town service anyway; there were much more direct routes. The only irritation stemmed from the viaduct position of Gospel Oak station. Passengers coming from the Barking direction and continuing westwards on the North London Line faced one long set of steps going down and another to go up again.

Both BR and the GLC were totally in favour of the change. However, this was an even more run-down service than the North London Line; the users' action group talked of the line going into: 'A kind of decaying limbo: trains were formed of hand-me-down stock with varying degrees of reliability, one by one the crumbling station canopies and buildings were demolished and replaced with basic structures and then progressively destaffed'.[30]

From 1980, services had been cut to just one an hour. However, after the service was diverted into the north platform at Gospel Oak, the service was increased to two trains an hour.

Returning to the Hackney diesel services, these were at least a start. But the reliability was poor, the trains did not run to an easy-to-remember service pattern, the old and noisy diesel units were a terrible advertisement for a modern train service, and all this undoubtedly affected usage in the first year, especially as promotion and understanding of the new service wasn't good.

Passengers simply will not use a service where reliability is poor if the off-peak interval is 30 minutes. The North London Line Committee had already warned[31] that 20 minutes was the absolute minimum service interval which could be accepted on an inner London service, while an internal warning came

---

30   http://www.barking-gospeloak.org.uk
31   North London Line Committee – *Hackney Line Diesel Services*.

on 28 March 1979 from the Eastern Region's director of engineering and surveying. Writing to the Liverpool Street divisional manager he said: 'Although it appears to be too late to influence the level of services for this coming year, I am firmly convinced that a 20-minute all day every day service is needed to revitalise the area and consolidate the future of the line'.

On 11 August 1980 – after angry queries from the GLC and Hackney Council on service reliability – the Eastern Region admitted: 'It is quite true that in the first 12 months of operation the service was not as reliable as we would have liked'. That at least was the draft reply to the GLC. The final version toned down the admission to put a more positive spin on the situation, saying that the problem was a chronic shortage of guards,[32] and adding that since May 1980, the recruiting position had greatly improved.

BR figures showed that in the week ending 29 March the cancellation rate was a staggering 13.9 per cent. Other bad weeks were the week ending 26 April when cancellations hit 8.9 per cent, that ending 17 May when it was 7.3 per cent, and the week ending 7 June when it was 11.7 per cent. However, reliability began to improve through June and July with the only real black spot being the week ending 19 July when 7.3 per cent of trains were cancelled.

Under pressure, the Eastern Region looked more closely into what was going on, and commissioned a remarkable report from Trevor Hill at the divisional manager's office in Liverpool Street, which pulled no punches in its analysis.

He found that in the first year of operation to May 1980, costs were £700,000 compared with revenue of £137,900. Thirteen per cent of trains had been cancelled, and almost two thirds of these cancellations were because no guard was available. Punctuality was never above 75 per cent and at worst was only 38 per cent. There was a lack of communication and 'very little control exercised by management on train operation' due mainly to the area manager at Liverpool Street being responsible for stations, while the area manager for Stratford was responsible for operating and signal boxes.

There was a lot more of this in a report which would have been dynamite to critics of the new service had it leaked out: 'There is in many cases very little notice of cancellation and it is often the case that train crews at Stratford will decide who runs what to where. Future sales and marketing plans will have limited effect if this fundamental point isn't improved'.

The new interchange at West Ham was ineffective as 'the trains' reliability is not satisfactory' while 'the station staff employed by London Transport do not consider that information to the public regarding BR operation is part of their job'. Hill found a definite relationship between the cancellations and the loss of revenue, showing that revenue dipped following a particularly bad run of service.

---

32   Not helped by a recruitment freeze slapped on in January 1980.

Custom House station 1979 with Brunswick power station in the background. The DLR transformed Custom House while the power station was knocked down in 1988.

Already there was a 'major problem of vandalism', which was not helped by the fact that for much of the time the stations were unmanned. The worst act of vandalism was the burning down of the up platform buildings at Custom House, and Hill reported that: 'At the time of writing (this) has not been rectified even though the incident occurred early in 1980. This delay created a very bad impression'. Unmanned stations in turn led to fare evasion problems: 'There is some evidence that fare evasion in this line is particularly high – a February 1980 survey found that 20 per cent of people had no ticket'. Matters did improve, but as late as 6 April 1981, the head of passenger operations still felt the need to impress on staff that trains must not leave early and instead stick strictly to the timetable.

Hill's detailed analysis – which contained a warning 'that this service has a distinct political flavour', reached Phillip Satchwell, passenger manager for BR London and South East. He agreed that there was a significant improvement in terms of reliability and usage, but he warned: 'Scope for growth is limited and we should start to think about economies, particularly if approval for electrification is not forthcoming next year'.

HAPTAC meanwhile, produced three cross-town linkline reports criticising BR for the lack of advertising and promotion of the service. Its discussions with

North Woolwich diesel unit at Highbury.

BR revealed that BR executives doubted whether a market really existed for the service – 'Show us the market' demanded David Kirby of BR.[33]

Everyone agreed that electrification of the line on the DC system was the way forward. Progress had been stalled while both the environment ministry and the GLC pondered how best to solve the transport problem in an un-regenerated Docklands without the inconvenient need to spend too much money.

At County Hall, the GLC planners were sitting on an estimate of £10.3 million – plus/minus 30 per cent – from British Rail to electrify the line. The GLC were keen to proceed; a cost/benefit study estimated that the diesel service would be expected to see daily passengers increase from 2,600 to 6,000. However, electrifying the section east of Dalston would be likely to increase this to 12,000.[34]

Traffic on the diesel service had grown fast already – between May and December 1980, daily usage was up by 16 per cent at Hackney Wick, 42 per cent at both Highbury and Camden Road, and 64 per cent at Hackney Central,

33 *Modern Railways*, July 1982.
34 The GLC study considered spending £5 million more and extending the line to Beckton, where housing growth was expected and which would probably have resulted in a higher traffic level. Some 20,000 people were expected to be living in Beckton compared to the 7,500 in Silvertown / North Woolwich. Trevor Hill's report thought that the commercial attractions of going to Beckton were 'far superior' to North Woolwich, adding that if this plan materialised, the North Woolwich section would probably close and a connecting bus service introduced. However, the Beckton service never happened.

admittedly from a very low base. And these increases did not include the traffic from the planned new stations at Homerton and Dalston Kingsland, which would be right in the middle of a major shopping area. However, traffic at Silvertown was only marginally up and at North Woolwich it actually fell by five per cent – stark testimony to the dire economic situation in the Docklands core.

All this was despite the background that the GLC was projecting that London's population would fall in the decade to 1991 by eight per cent – and by 14 per cent in the inner London boroughs.

There were five reasons for the predicted boom in traffic post electrification:

- Electric trains would be faster and more reliable. BR figures showed that an electric train took one minute from Highbury to Canonbury, but the elderly diesels took 2.5 minutes. Between Camden Road and Caledonian Road the timings were two and three minutes respectively.
- They could run a more convenient, regular interval service.
- They would be more modern and quieter and so generate a better pubic image.
- Instead of terminating at Camden Road they could run all the way to Richmond.
- They would run later in the evening.

The deliberations came as the economic situation worsened and the Conservative government was once again enforcing cuts in transport spending. In November 1980 the Eastern's chief passenger manager at York had warned that the worsening financial picture demanded cutbacks in the east London area diesel services, and said they would need to centre on the more generous peak hour provision. However he realised that the GLC would be 'extremely hostile' to this and cutbacks would jeopardise discussions regarding full scale electrification which he agreed was 'the only way to improve the line's finances in the longer term'. Instead he suggested that cuts should centre on the poorly patronised Stratford to Tottenham Hale service, and these were duly executed.

As late as 12 March 1981 an internal BR memo claimed: 'The GLC appear to be playing a game of brinkmanship as far as electrification is concerned' and they were told that the diesel service would be cut back if a decision was not reached soon. Finally, on 1 April, the GLC gave the formal approval to pay for the cost of electrification.

A British Rail revenue estimate on 20 January 1983 for electrification suggested that it would generate £0.73 million a year on a pessimistic view, and £1.3 million optimistically. As a key part of the programme, the ancient semaphore signals between Dalston and Stratford would be replaced by modern colour light signals, the two remaining signal boxes would be shut and the entire line controlled from the centre at Stratford.

The question remained of what to run the new service with. The obvious answer was to use the existing 1957 trains – four spare units were in store and could be refurbished in order to provide the additional capacity. However, the units already in service needed complete refurbishment and this was estimated to cost £55,000 per each three-car set. So it was decided to scrap them and replace them with surplus refurbished Class 416 (2 EPB) units from the Southern Region. This move had the operating advantage of motive power standardisation, since the 501 units were unique to the LMR DC electrified lines. But the main push for the decision came from the fact that they had already been replaced on the Euston – Watford DC line with new Class 313 stock, which would work on both DC and AC power.

With their replacement, there was already less work for the maintenance team at Croxley Green depot, and the complete withdrawal of the 501 stock would allow this depot to be closed, with maintenance switched to the Southern Region depot at Selhurst, near East Croydon. Eight 416 units would be needed for the line plus an extra three to cover for maintenance periods. Seventeen railwaymen lost their jobs at Croxley Green when the depot closed and £131,000 a year was saved in wage costs. The 416 trains were lighter than the 501 units at 70 tons instead of 100, and therefore more power efficient.

The accountants were therefore happy. The massive disadvantage for passengers was that they were made up of two-car units rather than three cars, and so there would be less room. This was thought not to be a problem. Internally, BR told its staff that 'original aspirations for traffic levels are unlikely to be realised in the foreseeable future due to the recession and slower than anticipated development of Docklands'.

The new electric service finally started on 13 May 1985, with all the Richmond trains now running to North Woolwich instead of Broad Street.

Even while the DC line was being built, planning was starting on a parallel AC overhead electrification to handle freight traffic more efficiently. In 1981, the government had approved the Anglia electrification to Ipswich and Norwich, and filling in the link between the GE line at Stratford and the West Coast line at Camden was an obvious move; it would allow through electric running between the lines resulting in greater operating efficiency.

The project was sponsored by Colin Driver, managing director, freight, and the proposal to the BRB Investment Committee on 15 August 1984 said that the cost would be £12.9 million, with a break even point in 1991.

Electrifying this section on AC would eliminate 5,000 locomotive changes each year while 14 diesel locos would not need to be replaced. The apparently high cost was due to the number of overbridges on the line between Dalston and Caledonian Road, and to mitigate these costs, it was proposed to single the section between Canonbury and Caledonian Road.

The project dovetailed neatly with plans to divert some trains from the Gospel Oak to Barking route on to the North London. This meant more efficient electric haulage throughout, but it allowed the deferral ('for as long as possible') of bridge repairs between Gospel Oak and Barking.

On 8 November, transport minister David Mitchell gave the go-ahead for the work, agreeing that it represented value for money.

Twelve Freightliner trains from Felixstowe, Harwich and Tilbury could then be switched to electrical haulage all across London. Also benefiting were the two daily company trains from Ford Dagenham to Liverpool Garston, and the Speedlink train from Dagenham to Halewood in Liverpool. Of these, the Speedlink Halewood service, one of the two Dagenham to Garston trains, and the Tilbury to Garston freightliner would now run over the North London Line rather than the Gospel Oak to Barking link.

It soon became clear that the Canonbury Curve could be added to the scheme for less than £0.5 million, giving the Eastern Region the opportunity to use the new link to divert services from the ports to the Great Northern main line which ran via Ely. The tunnel section on the curve was too narrow to support two freight trains at the same time, and so to avoid complicated work it was decided to single this section too. Also electrified was the steeply curved link from the North London down to the Great Northern north of King's Cross.

By 1986, there was some grumbling from the LMR that the single-line section through Islington would inhibit growth of the line, but the project director, Don Heath, said that there was ample capacity and that any constraints would be felt further east between Dalston and Stratford. Also in 1986, InterCity announced that it would divert the Harwich to Glasgow boat train – the short-lived *European* – over the new route too.

The AC section went live in April 1988, a project executed impeccably. There was only one small cloud on the horizon, hardly remarked upon at the time.

The electrification further enshrined the practice of running freight trains to the Midlands and the North via London. Actually, this was historically appropriate – the North London Line had originally been built for freight from the ports and not for the benefit of passengers – but was this really the right thing to do? What would happen if and when there was more demand for passenger trains over this route? And was deferring bridge maintenance on the Gospel Oak to Barking route 'for as long as possible' not yet another case of short term thinking?

Dalston – electric from Broad Steet and North Woolwich diesel in platform.

1971–1986: 'HALF FORGOTTEN AND HALF DESTROYED'

In which we look at how the City link to Broad Street was sacrificed to the property development needed to pay for the Liverpool Street reconstruction

In 1964, the London Midland Region wanted a windfall gain from selling the Broad Street site. But by 1969 British Rail had moved on and was ready to start comprehensive redevelopment plans not just for Broad Street but for Liverpool Street as well. It hired property consultants – Jones Lang & Wootton, Matthews and Goodman, and Healey and Baker – to come up with proposals for a complete redevelopment of the site. Now it was proposed to use the profits from the sale of most of Broad Street to finance the complete redevelopment of next-door Liverpool Street.

Liverpool Street was pure Victoriana, a rabbit warren of platforms and buildings which made it expensive and inconvenient to operate. Not unreasonably, the Eastern Region wanted to build a modern station out of this. Unfortunately, British Rail was cash-strapped and couldn't afford to rebuild Liverpool Street. It is a remarkable fact in hindsight that the 1960s redevelopment of Euston, whatever the aesthetics of the result, was entirely a railway project, with no office block planted on top. It was the last major scheme of its kind, and if a modern Liverpool Street were to be built, the only solution was to use profits from the Broad Street site to provide the necessary finance.

The first architect's plans, from Fitzroy Robinson, imagined that none of the Victorian architecture would remain and a brand new concrete and glass building would be erected – Euston reincarnated in the City.

In 1971, BR announced that an application for a speculative Office Development Permit (ODP) would be submitted for 1.5 million square feet of office space, and only when armed with this could they to apply for full planning permission. The ODP application said that the new station would incorporate 'certain of the services which at present run into Broad Street by the construction of a high-level viaduct which would switch some of the Broad Street tracks.' A hotel would be built on the site of Broad Street station.

Reaction in the environment department to the sheer size of the scheme was aghast – one minute in summer 1971 describing it, in easily understandable terms for its civil service readers, as: 'Pretty fantastic, the equivalent of three Marsham Streets'.[35] The civil servants were unsympathetic – they had already blocked a private sector scheme for 900,000 square feet of offices at the old Whitbread brewery site on Chiswell Street, and they failed to understand why a nationalised industry should be treated any differently.

---

35   The vast government office block off Victoria Street.

Liverpool Street was bound to be a highly political scheme. At the time the GLC was against further office development in Central London although the consequent shortage meant that rents were rising fast and jobs were relocating elsewhere. The GLC was not the only planning authority involved in the scheme either – there was also the City Corporation, while much of the Broad Street site fell under Hackney Council.

Property speculation was a political hot potato at the time given the large numbers of people on council house waiting lists, and ministers were desperate to avoid another embarrassment, with the footprint of a nationalised industry on it to boot. The year before, environment minister Peter Walker had threatened Harry Hyams, a controversial property developer, with government action if he continued to let four blocks, including Centre Point, remain empty. The building had been empty for six years, and the crazy state of the property market led to accusations that he was allowing it to remain empty on purpose, accusations he vigorously denied.

So in March 1973 the DoE civil servants proposed to British Rail that it came back and apply for an ODP with substantial named tenants in order to remove the speculative element from the scheme. They would be happy to issue an ODP if BR could get tenants for 0.9 million square feet of the proposed space.

BR had in fact already been negotiating with possible tenants; it had talked to the Baltic Exchange, Chase Manhattan and Williams & Glyn's Bank. But it patiently explained to the civil servants that if they went for a specific named tenant, the tenant would require early completion, which couldn't be guaranteed given the multiplicity of planning interests involved, and worse still, it would remove the board's bargaining power when it came to rentals.

In its fight to redevelop Liverpool Street, British Rail had one important ally in environment minister John Peyton. He had observed the snail's pace of progress on the scheme and minuted on 7 May 1973: 'The ancient and awful ODP process has been the main but not the only problem – the powers of darkness must have contributed considerable influence'.

The fate of the North London Line trains into Broad Street was critical to the scheme. The service was static with little growth and the station was far too large for the services it handled. A key piece of the jigsaw fell into place in 1971, when the government gave the long awaited go ahead to BR's proposals to electrify the Great Northern suburban services, and project them over the Finsbury Park to Moorgate tube line. This was planned to complete in 1976, and when it did, platform capacity at Broad Street could be cut to the original 1965 plan of two platforms, serving only the Richmond trains and the peak hour service to Watford. In September 1974 the Eastern Region issued its closure notices for the services to Broad Street and Moorgate, and for the closure of King's Cross (York Road). The last trains into Broad Street from the Great Northern finally ran on Saturday 6 November 1976.

Broad Street exterior – hard to believe that it ever stood here...

Those archaic inter-regional rivalries were evident again as the ER and LMR discussed what to do with the unwanted North London Line trains in the new complex. Not unreasonably, the Eastern Region regarded this as its scheme. Liverpool Street was its station and it wasn't unduly concerned with what happened to the Richmond and Watford trains as long as they didn't somehow become their problem.

On 29 June 1972 the ER divisional manager at Liverpool Street said he was 'strongly opposed' to the proposals being discussed within BR to divert North London Line trains to the Eastern Region over a brand new curve which would need to be built over the disused Graham Road goods depot in Hackney. From there it would rise to join the ER lines on a steep gradient. He cited the traffic to be expected from a large new housing development near Bishops Stortford, adding that he already had a closure proposal in hand for the inner city stations at London Fields, Cambridge Heath and Bethnal Green to help speed traffic up on the approaches to Liverpool Street.

The Graham Road goods yard had been disused since 1965 and in the BR estates department's eyes, it was land not earning its keep. In June 1973 they warned that they would want to sell this site if it were not wanted for operational use, and Hackney Council would certainly be interested in acquiring it for housing. This was a hazard to the redevelopment project, and in August the site was formally returned to operational duty.

In July 1973, British Rail went back to the ministry with revised proposals – a scaled down development of 1.2 million square feet, new shops and a bus station, and two high-level platforms for the North London Line. The rest of Broad Street could then be sold but the services would remain the same. All looked set to go – but on 18 December the government announced a total freeze on the issue of new ODPs.

Once again the project was on hold. And while it was on hold, the Eastern Region was left with an operating headache at Liverpool Street, and the condition of Broad Street continued to deteriorate. Bob Dashwood of the BR Property Board told the DoE that Broad Street was in a state of 'near dereliction with no revenue incentive to justify any improvements'. Meanwhile, valuable City space on the site of the goods depot was used for car parking to the detriment of the railways' commercial interests.

While the plans were on hold, railway executives continued to ponder the fate of the unwanted North London Line trains.

A meeting on 7 November 1973 had already discussed three options to solve the North London Line problem:

- A permanent station at Finsbury Avenue, on the west side of the existing Broad Street site. This would provide no easy interchange with the tube, but surveys showed that 90 per cent of passengers walked from Broad Street to their final destination anyway.
- A high level station on the East side, which would provide a better integration with the new Liverpool Street.
- Shutting the line south of Dalston Western Junction, closing Broad Street completely, and diverting trains over the proposed Graham Road curve into Liverpool Street.

The LMR's thinking initially was to defend its rights, and keep to the high-level plan at Broad Street, exactly as per option four back in 1965. The LMR general manager said the Graham Road option was unacceptable as 'future patronage on the Broad Street route is very largely tied up with the time advantage on the route to the City'. He added that: 'Broad Street is not a station where passenger convenience should be subordinate to estate development'. For good measure, the chief planning officer for LMR added he would need three platform faces at the new station and not two.

While the internal debate continued, the redevelopment plan took a big step forward.

As we have seen, the Labour government which returned to power in February 1974 had (initially at least) a far more sympathetic approach to British Rail's problems. The new environment minister, Tony Crosland, reversed the Conservatives' approach to office development and said he supported 'treatment of BR as a special case, at least for Liverpool Street'. On 12 August 1974 he issued an ODP for 1.2 million square feet with 25 per cent of this reserved for small business users – a key GLC demand.

By this time it was clear that the board itself preferred the Graham Road option for the North London trains and planning began for this. There was continued concern from the Eastern Region over proposals from the engineers to build the curve on a gradient of 1 in 41, and in order to keep this gradient down, to use single track only.

The definitive analysis appeared in a 22 May 1975 proposal to the BRB Investment Board from both the railway and property sides of BR – its authors were Bob Dashwood, of BRPB, and David Bowick, now chief executive, railways, and a veteran of controversies concerning the North London Line. They discussed three options:

- Option one – solve the traffic congestion at Liverpool Street by refurbishing Broad Street and diverting some of the Great Eastern trains via Stratford and Dalston to terminate there. The disadvantages were major – it couldn't be associated with a property development, it was undesirable to send these trains to Broad Street anyway, while overhead electrification would be needed. This option would relieve pressure on Liverpool Street but at 'very substantial cost' – only the four acres of the site of the former Broad Street goods depot could be redeveloped.

- Option two – retain a high level presence at Broad Street. This had the disadvantage that it would displace 30,000 square feet of profitable office space, it would mean a longer rebuilding process, would involve retaining the viaduct south from Dalston, and cause a delay in realising estate revenue as the high level station would have to be built first.

- Option three – shut the North London Line south of Dalston and divert the trains over the Graham Road curve into the low level site at Liverpool Street.

Option one was ruled out immediately, and Bowick and Dashwood duly recommended that option three be pursued. This went before the Investment Board and was eventually approved.

The problem for North London Line passengers was that the Graham Road curve would take time to build, but once the redevelopment scheme was approved, it would need to start as soon as possible at the Broad Street site to realise cash. That meant that North London trains would have to terminate 600 yards up the line at Worship Street, where a temporary terminal would be built for the six years until Graham Road was built. This temporary station was to prove the worst sticking point for the entire project.

However, by June 1975, and after the headline proposals for redevelopment had been published, the LMR had changed its mind. A meeting note records that Geoff Huskisson, the LMR divisional manager at Euston, was horrified at the relative cost and inconvenience of diverting 'the sparse Broad Street traffic' into the new station. He thought that Broad Street should be closed without the Worship Street replacement and the Richmond to Broad Street service terminated at either Highbury or Dalston or merged with the North Woolwich service as per the *London Rail Study*.

The chief passenger planning manager was unconvinced and retorted that 80 per cent of grant aided services had a higher level of grant than the North London Line and that the grant more than covered the train running costs and about half of terminal costs.

Undeterred, Euston was soon asking the Eastern Region whether the new Great Northern electrics could handle 2,300 passengers per day more if the North London service was terminated at Highbury.

Feelers went out to the environment department civil servants who would oversee the inevitable public inquiry into the Liverpool Street scheme. But at a meeting on 3 September, closure plans were firmly rebuffed. Although the LMR's representatives insisted there was no business case to spend £1.5 million to maintain the service beyond Dalston, the civil servants were not impressed. Ken Peter of the DoE said it was 'quite wrong' to make plans which did not involve continuing the service as it was quite impossible to predict the result of a closure proposal.

'Moreover,' he warned, 'As we well knew the public support for the North London Line was formidable and well organised.' Any cutback was, 'A very difficult political proposition'; evidently a repetition of the 1963 to 1965 experience was more than Whitehall was prepared to stomach. The culture of official secrecy meant, however, campaigners did not even know that, by their very existence, they had actually prevented a closure proposal from even getting off the ground. That unequivocal rebuff from the DoE was enough. On 9 September the chief passenger planning manager laid down definitively that the new station must accommodate the North London trains.

However, Huskisson had escalated his views to the LMR general manager who agreed with him, writing, in turn, to the BRB, in January 1976 calling the DoE approach 'economic nonsense'. He got an encouraging reply from Henry Sanderson, executive director, passenger, at BRB who had 'considerable sympathy' for this view. But Sanderson then went on provide an education in political reality. Inevitably, he said, such a large scheme would need to negotiate the full planning cycle, and the government would need to call in the proposals for a thorough inquiry by planning inspectors. Sanderson's suggestion was to: 'Make it clear that we can divert the service in the way proposed and state that plans are being made for this to be done, we would thus avoid actually promising that the plans would in fact be implemented'.

Sir John Betjeman: fighter for Victorian Liverpool Street.

Behind the scenes another powerful figure had weighed in against the North London Line. He was Sir David Serpell, a senior transport civil servant in the run-up to the Beeching Report, and on one occasion he claimed to have been the person who actually persuaded Beeching to take the job. He became permanent secretary at the transport ministry in 1968 and retired in 1972, joining the BRB in 1974.

Files at Kew contain a fascinating note from Michael Harbinson, chief rail planning officer, to Sanderson. This records that during a presentation to the board about the scheme, Serpell 'had asked what were the chances of taking the service off. He (Serpell) wondered in the circumstances whether you would care to rank it as one of your 'dodgy' services'.

Serpell was then a little-known figure, but he achieved fame of a kind when he wrote the notorious 1983 rail review which proposed cutting down the network to just 1,630 miles.

Word of all this seems to have reached the ears of Sir Geoffrey Finsberg, Tory MP for Hampstead, who, as a local councillor, had supported the campaign to save the line in the 1960s. He wrote to BR chairman Sir Peter Parker asking for assurances. He was told that there would be a temporary station at Worship Street while the Graham Road curve was built, and that 'our intention is to continue this service with as little inconvenience to passengers as possible'. But behind the scenes, elements within BR continued to dream of shutting the North London at Dalston, and abandoning City-bound travellers to the unsatisfactory interchange at Highbury.

With the axe pending over Broad Street, observers began to find architectural merit in it, while the impact of the project on the historic Liverpool Street buildings was starting to horrify campaigners. The Liverpool Street Station Campaign, which numbered among its members Sir John Betjeman, Spike Milligan and Tory MP Patrick Cormack, had already succeeded in getting the western train shed at Liverpool Street listed building status in August 1975. But in 1981 the environment ministry refused to list Broad Street, citing as its reason the refusal of the GLC to list it back in 1975.

David Lloyd, an architectural historian, said: 'The main block is an impressive piece of architecture and estate done in the French and Italian precedent, with a strong cornice and particularly effective centre roofing', Save Britain's Heritage proposed a scheme where the building would be converted into shops and restaurants – the City's answer to Covent Garden – which would then retain part of London's Victorian cityscape. The group reckoned that the cost of conversion would be £2 million, but the scheme did not find favour.

Broad Street in fact was in a terrible state. Mark Girouard, a well-known architectural historian, called it 'half forgotten and half destroyed'[36] while Betjeman called it 'London's saddest station'. Almost all the commercial premises on the station were closed and often one solitary railman sufficed to supervise things. Rain poured in through holes in the roof leaving huge puddles on the concourse, while on the forlorn east side of the station vegetation sprouted luxuriantly from the abandoned trackbed. Yet all this decline was not inevitable, Girouard wrote: 'The eye of imagination can see what an agreeable place the concourse with its shops could become if it led to something more positive than a few windy platforms below broken down sheds'.

On 13 July 1976 British Rail submitted revised development proposals, with the Great Eastern Hotel and the Abercorn Rooms saved, and with £28 million chopped off the project costs. Peter Shore, who had replaced Crosland as environment minister, called in the proposals and a planning inquiry was set up. In February 1977, the planning inspector – John Dahl – reported on the scheme, approving outline planning permission for the site. The report, said *Building* magazine, was 'a victory for conservationists' with the new Liverpool Street protected from a Euston-like fate and the listed western trainshed remaining. But Broad Street station would be closed and demolished, and while this was happening North London Line trains would be terminated at Worship Street.

On 27 March 1979, Shore gave planning permission and listed building consent for about one million square feet of offices and 30,000 square feet of shops. The closure of Broad Street would follow the normal closure procedures in the 1962 and 1968 Transport Acts. Only then did the implications of the temporary station at Worship Street begin to sink in. While it would only be a third of a mile from Broad Street, that would be a very long one third of a mile in pouring rain, especially as the walk would negotiate the largest building site in Europe. And passengers would be expected to use this for four to six years.

So opposition began to mount. Planning inspector Dahl provided ammunition when he supported outline planning permission. His report (paragraph 157) read: 'It is the users of Broad Street station who come off worst. Not only would their trains be terminated well away from the present station, but when the development is complete their journey would take four minutes longer'. He suggested that BR look again at the possibility of keeping a high-level route.

36   'The Battle of Liverpool Street' – *Country Life*, 19 June 1975.

Anthony Grant, Tory MP for Harrow Central said: 'It may be 600 yards, but whichever way one looks at it, it is nearly half or a third of a mile. It is not fun in bad weather or in the rush hour. It is not fun if one is old and perhaps unsteady on one's legs. It will not be fun in the dark when all the development work is going on'.[37] In Brent the Greenhill Residents' Group wrote to their MP protesting at the changes to their service to the City: 'We feel,' they said, 'that British Rail should primarily run trains for the benefit of the public; property development by British Rail should take second place'.

Much of the Broad Street site fell within the borough of Hackney, which, unfortunately for BR, was precisely the borough most upset with the project. Hackney's original submission to the planning inquiry had been fairly muted, although it opposed the Graham Road plan on the grounds that it might want to use the spare land for housing. But by 1981, BR noted that Hackney was specifically linking the Broad Street closure with co-operation on highways and planning for the scheme.

Since 1978, Whitehall and Hackney Council had between them committed nearly £5 million through the inner city partnership for economic development and environmental improvement schemes and £1 million had already been spent in the Shoreditch area. The spending was badly needed – at 15 per cent, male unemployment in the borough was by now double the London average.

On 20 May 1981, Gordon Pettitt, the divisional manager at Liverpool Street, warned that public and political opinion in Hackney would be a major factor to consider. Writing to Robert Goundry, divisional passenger manager, he said that Hackney Council members perceived that the development 'benefited everybody but Hackney', adding that entirely unrelated train service cuts on the Great Eastern lines through Hackney Downs were 'rightly or wrongly perceived as reductions in services prior to closure'.

Discontent in Hackney was linked to the regular demands that the disused NLL stations at Shoreditch and Haggerston be reopened. Hackney Council was under particular pressure from Jeffrey Roberts, who, in October 1980, became the first Liberal Party councillor for Shoreditch in 49 years. His election reflected the strong feeling in the area that Shoreditch residents were getting a raw deal from the Labour Party majority on Hackney Council. The deindustrialisation of inner London had hit Shoreditch especially hard, and to add insult to injury, Shoreditch Town Hall on Old Street lay empty and disused while residents had to take the bus to Hackney for municipal services.

Roberts campaigned hard for the reopening of the two stations, something which did not fit in at all with BR's plans. A Liberal leaflet said: 'Passenger trains already run through the old Shoreditch station while people are huddled together in chilly bus queues outside. Hackney Council does not seem to be pressing the case of Shoreditch people for decent public transport'.

---

37 *Hansard*, 1 December 1982.

Hackney commissioned a report from transport consultants Martin Vorhees Associates which, unfortunately for campaigners, concluded that, even in social terms, reopening couldn't be justified and didn't justify a more detailed review of the situation. Undeterred, Roberts continued his attack on Hackney Council and its Labour majority. He told the *Hackney Gazette*: 'The estimated capital cost of some £1–2 million compares favourably with the £5 million – or £13 million with interest – that Hackney is to spend on a swimming pool at the Britannia Centre. Much as I admire swimming pools they will not transform the economy of Shoreditch'.[38]

HAPTAC fought back with *The Case for Shoreditch Church Station*, which argued that the Vorhees report was flawed as its section on reopening Shoreditch 'was secondary to the main objective of their report, which was to examine the possibilities for the Dalston to Broad Street line as a whole and which suffered from the general lack of information available'.

The Vorhees report was gratefully received at BR as it undermined another potential argument against the closure. On 15 December 1981, Alan Etherington, the project manager for the redevelopment, wrote to Pettitt: 'Mr Roberts' enthusiasm for reopening Shoreditch and Haggerston stations is, it appears, shared only by a limited number of those we have met during recent consultations. Hackney Council's own report does not support the reopening of these stations.'

Hackney was concerned that British Rail was not legally bound to build the curve at Graham Road at all, as the plan was first to cut the service back at Worship Street and only then build the curve.

It wasn't surprising that people suspected that the curve wouldn't be built at all. We have already seen the internal opposition within the London Midland Region, and a memo written on 21 July 1981 by the chief operations manager, marked 'confidential', and sent to the general managers of both regions, said that they had originally wanted to divert Watford services to Stratford and admitted: 'We still hope that in the event we shall be able to close Worship Street without the need to build the curve at Graham Road'.

Later in 1981 Simon Osborne in the BR legal department warned that BR should firm up its assurance that the Graham Road link really would be built if it wanted to avoid endless delays with the progress of the Private Parliamentary Bill which was needed for the redevelopment. He said, 'Rightly or wrongly, MPs and others suspect our motives with regard to Broad Street and the North London Line'.

On 20 November, the formal closure notice for Worship Street – Broad Street was published, and on 2 April 1982, BR chairman Robert Reid wrote to Hackney confirming that the temporary station would be provided, with the curve following in due course.

---

38   *Hackney Gazette*, 22 September 1981.

Meanwhile, the crucial figures for passenger usage were providing annoy-ingly contradictory results. Passengers at Broad Street had fallen by 32 per cent between 1971 and 1978 due mainly to the loss of the GN services.

Table five – daily passenger usage at Broad Street 1969–1981

1969	8,516
1977	4,371
1978	4,618
1979	4,547
1980	4,054
1981	3,081

But the continued declines in 1980/1981 coincided with a sharp economic recession, and so may have had nothing to do with declining usage *per se*.

A count on 1 December 1982 showed that usage was actually going up! There were 1,030 passenger journeys daily on the critical Dalston to Broad Street section, compared with 901 for 15 September 1982 and 690 for a week-day count in 1981. The reason was that in the aftermath of the House of Lords' ruling that the GLC's Fares' Fair scheme was illegal, fares soared across London Transport to the point where a single to Broad Street cost 20p, but a bus jour-ney cost 60p. Traffic then declined once London Transport's fares were stabilised.

On 26 January 1983, the minister agreed to the closure of Broad Street. He didn't make it conditional on building the Graham Road curve, but he did insist on BR providing a Worship Street to Broad Street shuttle bus service, as well as some improvements to the unsatisfactory interchange at Highbury. But he refused to order BR to provide a new subway linking the NLL platforms with the Victoria Line, which BR claimed would cost over £1 million.

Hackney Council's officials fought long and hard to save the Broad Street link. Alone of the four original petitioners (the others were Islington, Camden and Brent councils) against the Redevelopment Bill, only Hackney pursued theirs into the Committee Stage of the Commons in early 1983.

Apart from being a useful rail service, there were two other side issues con-cerning the borough. Firstly, a closure would definitely prevent any reopening of the long closed stations at Shoreditch and Haggerston to help with regenera-tion of those areas. More crucially there was the question of the fate of the viaduct south of Dalston after traffic was transferred to the Graham Road curve. The City link viaduct arches were home to a variety of small industrial firms, which when surveyed in 1981, employed 722 people – scarce working class jobs which south Hackney and Shoreditch badly needed.

Ernie Roberts, MP for Stoke Newington, told the Commons that the arches were let by British Rail at low marginal cost rents and only minimal maintenance was undertaken. He added that closing the line would 'Leave Hackney with a 1¼ mile long industrial and environmental problem, which requires comprehensive planned attention to internal repair, cleaning and improvement of the local environment of the viaduct'. What would happen to all this after closure?

Hackney's strategy to save the link was to approach the GLC with a request that the latter fund some sort of service into Broad Street. The GLC had always stressed that they regarded the fate of the service to Broad Street as a separate issue which had nothing to do with the funding of electrification on to North Woolwich. So Hackney got a favourable response in principle, and on 11 October 1982, the GLC floated the possibility with Alan Etherington.

He replied with a firm 'No' nine days later.

The GLC then lodged a formal objection to the closure proposal on the ground that it would be prepared to pay for a high-level link.[39] However, British Rail was unrelenting – there was to be no high level presence in the new station, and on 27 January 1983, David Kirby, the director of London & South East Services (later to be rebranded Network SouthEast), which encompassed all the London suburban services, with the old regional structure scrapped, reiterated this refusal to accept finance from the GLC.

The BR case was consistent throughout with respect to the need for a complete shutdown at Broad Street. An internal memo assessing the high-level option listed six issues, many of them interlocking:

- Extra parliamentary powers would be needed, and getting these could take another year and a half. The legal department had earlier explained that it was now too late to change the text of the bill.
- Extra engineering work would also be required, probably taking another year and adding another one and a half years to the project. There would be an extra delay of 3.5 years if the high level platforms were built from the outset.
- The resulting delay would adversely affect 163,000 daily users, of which only 4,000 used Broad Street.
- Delay would adversely affect the momentum of the project.

---

39   BR meetings with Fred Pooley, the controller of planning and transportation at the GLC in late 1975 and early 1976, suggested that the GLC's original concern had not been the fate of Broad Street but rather the possibility of extending the East London Line from its inconvenient and illogical terminal at Shoreditch over tracks which had been in place into Liverpool Street until 1966. The GLC paid for a BR feasibility study into this plan, which would have allowed Southern Region trains to run into the City. The study identified several serious technical hitches including lack of a DC fourth rail into Liverpool Street and the implications of running slam door trains through the Thames Tunnel. But what finished the plan was the fact that there was no net revenue benefit to the scheme – a criterion with which British Rail had to judge all new investment proposals.

- Having to provide high-level platforms would increase staff costs by £30,800 a year as extra staff would be required there.
- It would remove the operating benefits of providing an integrated low-level station where passengers could easily switch between services; trains could use different platforms as required, and it would lose the ability to link Liverpool Street into the West Coast main line AC network, which would even make it possible to use Liverpool Street as an emergency terminus.

Etherington had been assiduous in gathering detailed information on alternative solutions so that the board's executives would be armed with ready answers if cross-examined during the process of the Redevelopment Bill.

Why not maintain the viaduct, for example, shut Broad Street, and then bring the trains down into the low-level Liverpool Street? Wouldn't that solution please everyone? The engineers told Etherington that this would require trains to descend on a 1 in 27 gradient, a new bridge would be needed under Great Eastern Street, and while this work was executed, trains would have to terminate at Shoreditch, not Worship Street. Given the current fuss about Worship Street, the idea of terminating trains further up the line at Shoreditch ought to be enough to shut up the objectors, thought the engineers. On 9 November 1982 Etherington's team carried out a site visit to Shoreditch and Haggerston stations to assess the likely cost of reopening, on the basis that this information might be needed for the House of Lords' select committee in early 1983.

In due course, the Redevelopment Bill cleared its parliamentary hurdles and passed into law. Then, out of the blue in September 1983, BR dropped a bombshell. The temporary terminus at Worship Street, which BR admitted was 'inconvenient but unavoidable,' would be dropped from the scheme entirely, and instead of the Graham Road curve being provided at the very end of the project, it would now be provided at the beginning, so allowing trains to be diverted from Broad Street directly into Liverpool Street.

The decision was made possible because surplus Class 313 units from the Eastern Region would be made available to run the Watford to Liverpool Street service as well as Watford to Euston. These units were built for the Great Northern suburban electrification and were dual voltage, designed to operate on both overhead AC and third-rail DC current.

Using them meant that there was no need to electrify tracks into Liverpool Street on the DC system. It also provided a useful additional cost saving – £0.8 million on building Worship Street, and £0.6 million in providing the shuttle bus service. There was also the matter of four complete trains of the 501 stock kept at Croxley Green depot near Watford and which were to be refurbished for the North Woolwich electrification. Not doing this saved £375,000.

Facing page: The NatWest tower soars behind Broad Street.

Although they were more modern than the 501 class stock, the new Class 313 trains were also more power hungry. A 13 July 1983 memo to BR corporate planning noted that the six-car trains on the DC lines would have to be cut down to three cars as the power demand of a six-car 313 formation 'could not be economically met'. Running six-car trains would cost £400,000 a year for the Watford services and another £200,000 for the North London Line if longer trains were ever deployed there. To help ease overcrowding on the Watford line caused by this cutback, Bakerloo trains would again run beyond Queen's Park to Harrow, although not to Watford.

The decision to use 313 Stock into Liverpool Street suggested that the main problem was solved. The link would now be built. But the decision still didn't solve everything. The Watford service was peak-hour only – what would happen to the off-peak service once the Richmond trains were diverted to North Woolwich? Would north-west London lose a useful link to the City?

The GLC had offered to pay for a Camden Road to Broad Street shuttle service into Broad Street, but Broad Street wasn't going to be around much longer. Discussions continued between the GLC and BR over what form such a service would take and on 5 January 1983 the GLC offered to pay for high-level platforms at the new Liverpool Street.

Broad Street Nocturne – 16 November 1983.

However, there was a new factor now. Margaret Thatcher had grown tired of the GLC under Ken Livingstone and its continued and vocal opposition to her policies. Buoyed by a resounding re-election victory in June 1983, she moved to end the problem definitively. Not by the democratic method of winning control of the GLC at the next election – but by using her parliamentary majority to abolish it. An October White Paper called *Streamlining the Cities*[40] was published outlining the plans. The GLC was now on borrowed time, and the unlikely but very successful love affair between the GLC and BR was over.

By November 1984 Laurie Pavitt, still an MP in Willesden 20 years later, had heard that BR was not planning any off-peak service to the City from the North London Line. He wrote to Malcolm Southgate, the LMR's general manager, asking for clarification.

On 26 November, Southgate replied, reiterating BR's original objections to a continued high-level presence in the new station. But he admitted: 'A further factor which influenced us was that when the offer was formally submitted to us by the GLC, the legislative background raised questions as to the future powers of the GLC to continue funding on a capital or revenue basis.' He insisted that BR would still consider a shuttle as long as funding for it didn't erode its entitlement to Public Service Obligation grant from Whitehall.

The GLC, and especially its combative transport chairman Dave Wetzel, believed that BR had backed off under government pressure, and he went on to accuse BR of reneging on its offer. On the political right, Geoffrey Finsberg accused BR of 'gross deceit' over the affair. But the idea of any shuttle from Liverpool Street to the North London Line was dead. British Rail was close to achieving their project objectives, and with no GLC to worry about any more, it could be firmer in its insistence that the plans didn't stack up financially. On 18 January 1985, David Kirby wrote to Eric Midwinter, chairman of the London Regional Passengers' Committee (LRPC) – the body which succeeded the TUCC – saying that a shuttle to Camden Road would only benefit 6,000 people a week, 'a small number in railway terms' of which 79 per cent had a reasonable rail alternative. He said that trains running at a 20-minute interval would carry an average of only 15 passengers per train.

The abolition of the GLC in 1986 was a disaster for public transport as it scrapped the only strategic transport authority for the capital and it removed a key source of funding for capital schemes. The projection of the North London through Hackney and on to the North Woolwich line would not have happened without the support of the GLC (partially under Tory control in fact!). The reopening of the link between Farringdon and Blackfriars, closed to passenger traffic in 1916 and to goods in 1969, made possible the Bedford to Brighton Thameslink service. Although BR was convinced of the cost benefits of this scheme, it would never have happened were it not for an initial £50,000

---

40   *Streamlining the Cities*, 1983 Cmd 9063.

The concourse at Broad Street.

feasibility study paid for by the GLC, and another £100,000 to keep the scheme going, the latter paid just before the GLC lost the power to vote money for transport schemes. The abolition of the GLC delayed for 10 years the re-launch of a passenger service on the West London line from Clapham Junction on to Olympia and Willesden Junction.

BR duly raised a new closure proposal to shut the entire stretch from Broad Street to Dalston Western Junction once the Graham Road curve was built. BR already had approval to shut Broad Street, but this new proposal was needed because its lawyers believed that a proposal covering Dalston to Worship Street might be illegal, as Worship Street didn't yet exist! So BR issued a new Section 54 notice – giving notice of its intentions – on 1 March 1984.

There was a delay in issuing the next stage of the closure formalities – the detailed Section 56 notices – because the wording of these had already been challenged by the objectors to the massively controversial plans to shut the Settle and Carlisle line. The objectors to the Settle and Carlisle closure discovered[41] that the wording BR habitually used for Section 56 notices was not actually in accordance with the 1962 Act in its definition of who would be affected by a closure and who could object to it.

---

41   See Towler, James: *The Battle for the Settle and Carlisle*, 1990.

The famous lombard staircase at Broad Street.

The North London Line Committee – always slightly dubious about the cross rail link to North Woolwich as its main base of support was among Hampstead users who valued their City link – grumbled about the GLC's 'perverse' decision in paying for the North Woolwich electrification without securing a guarantee from BR about the fate of the Broad Street service. It called the Graham Road connection 'wasteful' and, with some prescience, its newsletter warned that 'Watford trains are likely to be given a low priority amongst Liverpool Street services'. As it turned out, the NLLC would be proved right – but for the wrong reason.

Preparations for the rundown continued; train drivers from Broad Street tipped off the NLLC that BR was moving the crew depot and signing-on point from Broad Street to the much less convenient Stonebridge Park, and as a result, from 1 October 1984, two of the Watford to Broad Street trains would be cut.

The closure proposal went before the LRPC, which had received objections from 61 local organisations and 231 individuals, including members of the NLLC and HAPTAC. The submission from HAPTAC complained that property redevelopment was defining transport provision and not the other way around, noting that BR had failed to provide any evidence of low or declining usage for the service.

The LRPC report was a slap in the face for BR and recommended that the government refuse the closure proposal. It said it was: 'Undeniable that there would be hardship if Broad Street, Dalston Junction and the connecting lines were closed. Unlike almost every other closure case, where lines and stations are suffering from underuse, the figures reveal a service which is reasonably buoyant and viable.' However, the Committee found it hard going to disentangle the row between BR and the GLC, saying that the fact that BR and the GLC 'indulged in so perplexing a saga of offers, acceptances and retractions indicates a disturbing level of confusion'.

John Sanderson remains convinced that 'we won the transport case' but unfortunately the basis of official decision making had nothing to do with transport in this case and there was no chance whatsoever of the LRPC's recommendation to save the line being accepted. BR needed cash to rebuild Liverpool Street, and by good fortune was sitting on a pot of gold which could finance it, with Broad Street station being in the right place at the right time.

Computer technology meant that City firms no longer needed to be right on the doorstep of the Bank of England, Lloyd's or the Stock Exchange. There was actually a surplus of City office space, but it was all old – there was a huge demand for new accommodation suitable for this new way of working with large open plan offices and trading floors linked by underfloor cabling being essential. The replacement complex – to be called Broadgate – was just what the rapidly changing financial firms in the City were waiting for; full deregulation of the Stock Exchange (Big Bang) was on the horizon now and the new space would be badly needed.

Broadgate would spread over 32 acres, and was easily the largest development in the City since the war. The developers had to limit Broadgate to being a medium rise project due to a planning restriction that the view of St Paul's Cathedral's dome from Richmond Hill should not be obstructed by offices on the skyline behind the cathedral,[42] and this naturally affected the value. When fully staffed it had the somewhat counter-intuitive result of making Union Bank of Switzerland easily the largest private sector employer in Hackney (until boundary changes in 1994). It was also one the pioneers of privatised City space – although hordes of people pass through it daily, almost all of them are unaware that they have no legal right of way as this is private property patrolled by its own security guards with access only by concession.

42   *Modern Railways*, April 1986.

The Broadgate complex remains a symbol of the brash 1980s' City culture, and listed building status was refused in 2011 after lobbying from the City; it may need to be completely knocked down and rebuilt someday.

By this time BR had a new partner for the scheme. Instead of a Wimpey and Taylor Woodrow consortium as the developers with Fitzroy Robinson as architects, it was now Stuart Lipton's property company Rosehaugh Stanhope as developers and Arup as the architects. BR was under pressure to sign the contract with Rosehaugh Stanhope so that the demolition and building work could start. With Broad Street still in place, no matter what the hardship for passengers, then the Liverpool Street redevelopment could not happen. So on 19 April 1985, the closure of Broad Street and Dalston Junction was approved by environment secretary Nick Ridley. They would finally close as soon as the Graham Road curve was ready. With the electrification to North Woolwich complete, the Richmond service was diverted there from 13 May 1985 and only the peak hour Watford service remained.

That just left the fate of the viaduct to be decided. One proposal was to use it as an express busway. London Transport was not keen, citing the need for passengers to climb a lot of stairs, and it suggested an express roadway instead. There was also talk of a light railway service running along the viaduct but as this could only run from Dalston to Worship Street the idea didn't last long. A GLC study suggested that the express busway was the only option which covered the costs involved.

Hackney did get one consolation prize. In return for various planning permissions, BR agreed to pay for the reopening of London Fields station, on the Liverpool Street to Enfield Line. This had closed after fire damage in November 1981 – another Inner London arson case – and it duly reopened in 1986.

The final version of Liverpool Street was universally regarded as a success story. It provided 18 platforms, which was not actually an increase. But they were lengthened, meaning that two trains could occupy one platform if required. The station was nicely integrated into one whole, while brand new entrances to the tube were provided along with a bus station. A more ambitious proposal to increase the number of platforms to 22 was rejected on cost grounds. The entire project was designed to leave the BRB with a surplus of £20 million,[43] but the final outcome was much more impressive than that. A project report dated September 1992 showed that estimated spending on railway works, mainly Liverpool Street itself but also including Graham Road, was £152 million. But the Broadgate development had been increased in scope to include buildings both on Bishopsgate, and on the site of the viaduct immediately to the north of Broad Street. This meant that the board's income from the development was predicted to be £415 million, leaving a surplus of £263 million – profit which was not reinvested in the North London Line.

43   *Modern Railways*, April 1986.

1986–1992:
'GROTESQUE FIGURES INDEED'

In which we look at the last days of Broad Street station, recall a long forgotten visit by a former Beatle, and plunge into a classic 'closure by stealth' row.

With the fate of Broad Street all but sealed – the station finally made it on to the big screen with the release of Paul McCartney's film *Give My Regards to Broad Street* which also featured Ringo Starr. There wasn't really much of a plot to it, but it gave McCartney the chance to showcase some new songs including the number one hit *No more lonely nights*.

McCartney later said: 'That station was like fate. It was waiting for us. I'd been searching in my mind for a title for a film and liked the idea of a parody on *Give My Regards to Broadway* – a New Yorkerish title that I could give a London twist to. When we filmed at Broad Street station, I knew I'd got it. It's a nice feeling when things happen naturally like that.'

The film does indeed capture the atmosphere of Broad Street in its final years. In one of the final scenes – stunningly done – McCartney wanders on to the dimly lit and deserted concourse late at night. Puddles dot the pavement. In a corner a wino sits drinking against the peeling paintwork. A man kisses his girlfriend goodnight as she disappears on to the platform and the camera watches him vanish down the Italianate staircase towards the street.

Cut to a 501 class train departing into the azure London night and a solitary railwayman walking home across the concourse, his shift over. Then McCartney squeezes through the half-closed barrier gates and wanders along the rain-soaked platform where the puddles reflect a ribbon of light from the platform lamps above. To his left a train is darkened and locked up for the night; to the right, the effect of lamplight and rain provides a mist like effect over the luxuriant vegetation on the closed down eastern platforms and McCartney stretches out on a platform seat to think. Allegedly,[44] the production team later returned for a retake of the scene, spending hours on a summer night hosing down the platforms to ensure they were as damp as the original sequence. Roger Lansdown of HAPTAC saw some of the filming and even wrote to McCartney asking for his support to keep the station open.

Despite costing around US $9 million to make, the film was not a success and today is remembered only by a certain few of a certain generation. Pretty much like Broad Street station in fact.

Once closure was approved by Nick Ridley in April 1985, on condition that it didn't take place until the Graham Road curve was operational, things moved quickly. A month later, the Richmond services ceased to use the station. There would only be a handful of passengers from now on.

---

44   http://www.signalbox.org/branches/jh/broadstreet2.htm

The demolition teams moved in – there was no time to waste if the new offices were to go up. The track was quickly lifted, the remaining tenants of the commercial premises at ground floor level and on the concourse itself departed. The stone obelisk war memorial, which had stood on the concourse since the end of the First World War, was carefully dismantled. It later found a home at Richmond station before being relocated to the one at Hoxton.

From Monday 1 July, the main access was closed and access became through a narrow opening in Sun Street Passage. A tatty pair of makeshift wooden double doors carried a BR notice saying that the station was open from 06.45 to 10.00 and from 16.00 to 18.30 Monday to Friday, and closed at weekends.

Once through the door, passengers had to climb a scaffold type enclosed wooden staircase which led to a covered walkway across the platforms to the remaining two platforms. These were platforms three and four which were renumbered two and one and moved northwards. A wooden temporary ticket office had been established with a small waiting area and minimal staff facilities. Another path then led to the bare and exposed platforms. It is a wonder that any passengers were prepared to use such miserable facilities.

Some mystery concerns the fate of the superb Italianate staircase up to the platforms (as illustrated on page 101), which was carefully dismantled and moved to secure storage at a railway arch at Stepney East. It was hoped that these pieces could be re-used somewhere – but a year later the pieces were found to be stolen and have never been recovered.[45]

The station's long life ended with the last Watford departure on Friday 27 June 1986. By then, much of the western part of the site, on the grounds of the Broad Street goods depot, was already built over and staff had moved into the new offices. To this day, Broad Street remains the only main line London terminus to have been closed.

BR discovered that the high cost of maintenance they had previous raised as a problem with maintaining the Broad Street service actually referred only to the track and signalling, and the physical structure of the viaduct itself was safe and secure. The viaduct ownership was offered to Hackney Council for a nominal sum, and the scores of small business working underneath the arches could carry on their work without even the occasional rumble of the peak hour Watford trains overhead.

The closure meant that another piece of unused railway land had been added to the cityscape just as transport planners were trying to bring these back into use again. With the scrapping of proposals to bring the East London Line into Liverpool Street, London Transport began to investigate linking the East London with the North London over the disused viaduct to provide a completely new service. But it would be almost 25 years before trains were to run across this viaduct again.

---

45   *London Railway Record*, January 1995.

The remaining Watford services – operating on Monday to Friday peak hours only – were then diverted to Liverpool Street over the Graham Road curve. The service was not a success; the trains were slow and plagued by cancellations and unreliability and were gradually removed to the point – after May 1990 – where there was only one train in each direction.

Ken Livingstone, reincarnated as an MP in Brent after the abolition of the GLC, raised the growing threat to the service in the Commons, asking the government to exert pressure on BR to 'prevent the closure of Primrose Hill station, because it is BR's clear intention now to reduce the number of trains running on the Watford line to Liverpool Street, from five an hour to one an hour'.[46]

On 9 October 1990 Chris Green, who had succeeded David Kirby, asked for BRB approval to start closure proceedings. He said that the one remaining train was, 'employing resource which could be used to better effect elsewhere'. He expected closure to lose £30,000 a year in revenue, but thought that would be easily made up by the deploying the set elsewhere.

The following table shows clearly how the service had been allowed to deteriorate.

Table six – passenger figures for the Liverpool Street – Watford service

Date	Number of trains	Number of passengers	Average per train
July 1986	13	392	30
Nov 1987	10	389	39
Nov 1988	8	271	34
Nov 1989	4	100	25
Nov 1990	2	63	31
Nov 1991	2	36	18
The November 1989 figure is an estimate as figures are available for two trains only			

On a sample weekday in April 1991, said NSE, only 66 passengers used the train from Liverpool Street and only 21 got on or off at Primrose Hill.

The LRPC hearing into the closure took place on 31 October 1991 and was a classic 'closure by stealth' debate. The rules of closure by stealth are as follows:

1. Decide on the railway line you wish to close.
2. Reduce the level of services.
3. And/or make them less convenient to use, in terms of connections for example.

---

46   *Hansard*, 12 June 1989.

Last day at Broad Street – 27 June 1986.

4. Watch passengers drift away.

5. Then apply to close the service citing declining use.

This is what exactly what happened in the case of the Settle and Carlisle line. When it came to the last North London Line service to Watford:

- NSE said that patronage on the service had been declining for several years and had the figures to prove it. *This*, they said, was why the service had been progressively reduced.
- Objectors – 74 of them[47] – said lower usage was precisely *because* the service had been cut back and because reliability was so poor.
- Between 1 January and 16 May 1990 there had been 32 cancellations of the morning service, and 34 in the evening.

During the hearing, news filtered in that BR had just announced that the 17.50 to Watford had been cancelled again due to the lack of a guard. The LRPC report recorded that the news 'was received with laughter'.

NSE accepted the poor reliability record, but argued that if there were problems elsewhere on the North London Line then cancelling the Liverpool Street trains 'inflicted the least inconvenience overall'. It proposed to use the train released by the closure to run an extra service on the increasingly overcrowded

---

47 An admittedly very low figure – it might have been higher if passengers had not drifted away from the terrible service, of course.

Five years after – post closure ruin at Dalston Junction, 1991.

Stratford – Hampstead Heath – Richmond section. The closure was not, they said, a cost saving exercise but a 'better use of resources' given 'finite rolling stock resources'.

The LRPC was not impressed. Its report recommended that the minister refuse closure consent saying that 'British Rail have treated users of this service disgracefully over a long period, with progressive reductions in service and frequent cancellations of the remaining trains', adding that the cancellation of the train on the day of the hearing itself was 'symptomatic of BR's cavalier attitude'. The LRPC secretary openly accused NSE of pursuing 'closure by stealth'.

However the transport secretary approved the closure and the last train ran on Friday 25 September 1992, finally ending north-west London's direct link to the City. Primrose Hill station was also closed from that date, although due to flooding, the last train didn't actually call there, travelling via Hampstead Heath instead.

That wasn't quite the end of the affair though. On 22 October, transport minister Roger Freeman wrote to NSE. Referring to cancellation rates of 34 per cent (morning) and 51 per cent (evening) between November 1991 and July 1992, he called them 'grotesque figures indeed' and complained that reducing the service during a closure programme only gave ammunition to critics who claimed that a closure by stealth programme accompanies every closure proposal.

For NSE, John Nelson, who had succeeded Chris Green as managing director,

Jonathan Roberts.

Stephen Joseph.

replied insisting that there really was no closure by stealth activity although he accepted that many customers might have thought there was. He reiterated the 'stark choices' faced by operations teams dealing with unreliable trains who, at short notice, had to cancel either a Euston train or a Liverpool Street one at times of train failure. He promised that a reliable service would be run during any future closure proposal.

Nelson, of course, was in a no-win situation. The reason why staff had to make short notice cancellation decisions was because they lacked enough trains to run a proper service. The Class 313 stock was now 15 years old and was becoming less reliable as time went on. With no stock on standby, it did make sense to prioritise the Euston service. And that lack of rolling stock was entirely due to government underfunding over a period of years and the pre-privatisation chaos. But Nelson obviously couldn't say that to the minister.

The Graham Road curve, which cost £2.5 million, occupied so much time and generated so much heat, is now only used for empty stock movements from the Liverpool Street lines towards Hornsey Depot. But it may be regarded as a good investment when set against the profit BR made from the demolition of Broad Street, of course.

No trace of Broad Street station remains amid the Broadgate development and it takes some imagination to realise that a huge railway station once occupied this site. The only clue can be seen by travellers from Liverpool Street who, if they look carefully to their left immediately on leaving the station can see the overgrown and crumbling remains of the viaduct which once carried the Broad Street line. That, and a plaque on the Broadgate development in memory of the three firemen who died fighting a blaze at the Broad Street Goods Depot late in 1951.

At Primrose Hill, the surface buildings were let as commercial premises and the stairs removed but at platform level the buildings were mothballed and the substantial Victorian canopy remained in situ. The station was demolished on 6 December 2008, despite the efforts of local conservation groups to save it. Once Camden Council decided that it had no interest in the site, the demolition crews moved in, although the tracks remain and freight trains, along with diverted passenger trains, continue to pass through today. Network Rail claimed that the buildings were in a dangerous condition and had to be demolished to stop debris falling on to the track.

The demolition was also despite Transport for London's on-off thoughts about a Stratford to Queen's Park service. Such a service might imply stopping the local Euston to Watford service completely and restarting Bakerloo trains all the way to Watford. Most passengers from the Watford direction switch to the Bakerloo at Queen's Park anyway, and traffic from the two stations further in – Kilburn High Road and South Hampstead – towards Euston was relatively light as more direct routes to central London existed. These stations might be more useful as part of an orbital route.

1983–2007: 'SHABBY, UNRELIABLE, UNSAFE, OVERCROWDED'

In which we look at the unhappy experience of railway privatisation, when passengers discovered what happened when systematic underfunding coincided with rapid traffic growth.

On 1 October 1989, the class 416 trains were replaced by the three-car class 313 stock. With the last run of 416 stock, the era of slam door trains on the line had come to an end. No more would the line hear the familiar CLOP, CLOP, CLOP of the doors being slammed all down the train as passengers alighted and trudged home along a freezing platform at Canonbury or Finchley Road.

Entirely genuine health and safety concerns had been rising for years over slam door carriages[48] and, on paper, the Class 313s were a big improvement on the 416s. They had a more modern appearance and were a better advertisement for the service; they provided a 50 per cent increase in capacity, although this only restored the situation to that offered by the old 501 class units which had been scrapped to save money.

The problem lay in the fact that they had only two sets of sliding doors per car. This apparently trivial design feature mattered because, from 1983, the unexpected happened. Against all the predictions, Greater London's population stopped falling.

A falling population underlay all railway planning assumptions, including, as we have seen, the *London Rail Study* of 1974, the BR opposition to the reopening of Kentish Town West, the 1981 GLC cost/benefit study for electrification to North Woolwich, and the decision, taken when population falls had already ceased, to substitute the two-car 416 class trains for the three-car 501 units.

Between 1961 and 1983, London lost a million people, or 15 per cent of its total population, From the 7.8 million logged in the 1961 census, it declined steadily to reach a low of 6.73 million in 1983. Depopulation was greatest in inner London – where, apposite to this study – Camden and Hackney both lost 29 per cent of their people while Islington lost 38 per cent.

But after 1983, the population began to rise steadily again, reaching 6.9 million in 1996 and 7.3 million in 2001. There were several explanations. Firstly, London living was becoming more interesting again compared to the perceived dreariness of suburbia. Commuting was – even then – becoming tiresome and expensive. The UK's internal brain drain means that, each year, thousands of young people come to London to study and most of them stay to benefit from the greater career opportunities in the Big City. Then too there was foreign immigration, both rich and poor.

---

48   There were in fact 165 deaths from moving trains between 1981 to 1990.

This population growth was disproportionately high in the inner boroughs. The pundits who feared that a fate similar to that of Detroit lay in wait for Britain's inner cities, with a central business zone surrounded by a dangerous, poverty stricken and mostly black inner city, with the white population fleeing to suburbia for safety, had got it wrong.

The phenomenon of gentrification – middle class couples buying up cheap and unwanted property in the inner cities on a scale large enough to change the entire character of a neighbourhood by its refurbishment – meant that sections of the inner city were becoming attractive again.

So while the population of Greater London rose by eight per cent between 1983 and 2001, adding the entire population of a Leeds or a Sheffield in so doing, that of the gentrified inner London boroughs served by the North London Line rose by significantly more. The population increase here was 11 per cent in Camden, 13 per cent in Hackney, and 16 per cent in Islington.

It followed that this was more a middle class population too. Taking owner occupation as a proxy for social class, we find that in the 1980s, owner occupation grew by 60 per cent in Inner London as a whole, which was impressive enough. But it grew by 80 per cent in both Hackney and Islington.

Gentrification fed on itself too. As London recovered from the housing price crash which bottomed out in 1994, the years to 2000 saw average Greater London property prices jump by 96 per cent. But the increase was 103 per cent in Islington, 105 per cent in Camden and 116 per cent in Hackney, while outer London boroughs saw much lower increases. By January 2014, Land Registry figures showed that at £526,361, average property prices in Hackney had become the seventh most expensive of all the 33 London boroughs.

Throw in the facts that:
• People were expected to travel longer distances to work
• They often had to cross London too
– and the result was that the North London Line traffic grew quickly.

Taking 1985 as a baseline, the number of passenger journeys was up by 8.5 per cent in 1986, 14.5 per cent in 1987, 36.1 per cent in 1988, and 53.9 per cent in 1989. Traffic growth then stagnated along with the economy, but unlike most routes, traffic did not fall, and by 1993, the growth figure compared with 1985 was 60.9 per cent.[49]

The 313 class units were totally ill-equipped to handle this increased traffic, given that the line's defining feature was 'the intense traffic flows similar to a bus service', as the LMR's researchers had noted back in 1965.

There were only three trains an hour, and with their limited door space, huge scrums built up on platforms at the evening peak hour. Passengers already on the train and only going a few stops further, stayed firmly put near the carriage doors, afraid that if they followed staff exhortations (often with megaphones)

---

49   *Modern Railways*, February 1994.

Silverlink days: scrum in the evening – Highbury, 2005.

and 'moved right down inside the car' they would be trapped and unable to get off at their stop. The result of this crowding was that more passengers could not get on, even though there was theoretically standing space within the train. Tempers snapped frequently and fights were by no means unknown. Louise Banham, who travelled from her home in Highbury to her office in Camden Town, said 'I feel like a sardine packed into a tin – it is a really revolting experience'.[50] Time spent loading and unloading, which wasn't allowed for in the timetable, then caused further delays.

The eastbound platform at Highbury in the evening peak was a particular horror, with streams of Hackney-bound commuters changing from the Victoria Line and being unable to board despite the activities of station staff. The westbound platform at Canonbury was a similar nightmare in the morning peak as the trains were then full of passengers who had boarded further east, many of whom would detrain at Highbury.

---

50   *Highbury and Islington Express*, 17 July 1998.

The extent of the overcrowding was only quantified years later. By March 2006, the westbound morning peak trains, covering the three busiest hours, had official space for 5,120 passengers: but with 3,712 sitting, and 1,745 standing, this was 337 in excess of capacity. That meant that on leaving Stratford the seats had all been taken, and after Dalston, each train had become a travelling sardine can.

These figures are probably an underestimate; a London Assembly report on railway overcrowding[51] noted that published overcrowding figures were skewed because crowding was measured over a three-hour peak. But the worst over-crowding was actually compressed into a relatively narrower time period, both in the morning and afternoon.Things eased somewhat after the train passed Highbury, but seats would still not become available until after Camden Road.[52]

Official figures do not really capture the sheer vile unpleasantness of being one of those sardines, fighting to get on, fighting to get off, squashed far too close against someone on a steamy summer evening on a non-air-conditioned train.

The trains themselves were a depressing experience even in the off-peak period. The carriages never seemed to be cleaned often enough, the windows were grey and scratched, and a stale musty smell lurked inside. (The operator blamed 'the lack of robust access to carriage washing machines … (which) … contributes to a poorer level of presentation than the service demands'.)

The overcrowding was exacerbated by the worsening reliability. By 1994, the North London Line had more cancellations than any other line in the entire South East of England – at 3.5 trains for every 100. And it was one of only three lines which were actually getting worse.[53] John Sanderson, by now the secretary of the North London Line Committee, complained that of 40 journeys to work he made, there were two double cancellations (where successive trains did not run), four single cancellations, and two complete breakdowns of service.

Sometimes passengers' frustration boiled over. One February morning in 1996, passengers waiting at Camden Road for the 07.45 to Willesden were told that it had been cancelled. The next train was not until 08.21. A passenger told the local newspaper what happened next: 'People got fed up of waiting and when another train pulled in they got on and demanded to be taken to Willesden. When they were told the train was terminating here they just refused to get off'.[54] The police had to be called to dislodge the angry passengers.

The next year, the annual report of the LRPC said the NLL had highest can-cellation rate of any London operator, which the committee blamed on the 'antiquity and mechanical unreliability of some of the rolling stock'.

---

51   *The Big Squeeze, Rail Overcrowding in London*, February 2009.
52   Network Rail, *Route Utilisation Strategy for Cross-London Traffic*, 2006.
53   *Highbury and Islington Express*, 31 March 1994.
54   *Hampstead and Highgate Express*, 16 February 1996.

The squeeze on passengers played out against the background of railway privatisation. By the early 1990s, railway insiders knew full well that the North London Line was a thoroughly clapped out railway requiring substantial new investment. Network SouthEast wanted to ease overcrowding by increasing the passenger trains from three an hour to four an hour yet it was also facing a huge new demand from the freight expected to arrive via the Channel Tunnel and Stratford and bound for Willesden.

A status report on the line, dated 4 July 1991 and written as part of the analysis of evolving freight requirements, said the line was 'not well constructed, has been severely neglected at times over the years and much of it is in poor physical condition'. The DC system west of Dalston was 'completely life expired' while that to the east, financed by the GLC, and only six years old, was only just adequate. This report recommended that the whole line be re-electrified on the AC system.

At NSE, Chris Green saw the report and commented: 'We clearly need to prepare a total route modernisation paper for the North London Line for inclusion in the 1991 Rail Plan'. But soon, NSE was in difficulties itself; it had made huge strides under Green, traffic was up and need for PSO subsidy was down. But in December 1989, transport minister Cecil Parkinson confirmed that he wanted NSE's £90 million subsidy to end by 1992–93. Lower subsidy for NSE was already set as a BRB target – but the following winter, Britain fell into recession. Living without subsidy in a recession had to mean rising fares with life-expired assets not being replaced.

Cuts were inevitable. During the winters of 1991–92 and 1992–93 there was no North London Line Sunday service at all because of maintenance work – but NSE refused to pay for a replacement bus service.

Destaffing of stations all across the capital gathered pace, leading to a sharply critical report – *Get Staffed* – from Eric Midwinter at the LRPC. NSE executives were adamant during what the LRPC called 'tense discussions' that the short-term benefit of saving on staff costs outweighed the long-term damage this was doing to passengers' perceptions of the railway.[55]

Against this gloomy financial background, an options review for the NSE 1992 Rail Plan listed several financial options with varying degrees of cutbacks. The baseline option, to operate within the Established Financial Limit laid down by Whitehall, predicted that

- Some structures could become unsafe leading to closures.
- Cleaning standards would fall significantly (exterior by 80 per cent and interior by 50 per cent).
- There would be a significant risk of closure of diesel services (including Gospel Oak – Barking) after 1996 due to fleet age.

---

55   London Regional Passengers' Committee annual report 1992–93.

Under this worst case scenario, the NLL had another narrow escape – the 1992 Rail Plan noted that under the baseline case 'funding (had been) included to stop closure of the North London Line (£10m over five years)'. An NSE document explained 'North London Line bridge renewals are an example where NSE on its own would close the route, but we recognise the corporate need, because of its importance for freight, and have provided for renewal'.

In the dying days of Network SouthEast in October 1993, a report called *Expanding the Horizons* listed possible service improvements. It was distributed to local councils along the route under the auspices of David Watters, NSE North divisional director, and the man who would be managing director of the shadow company pre-franchising. *Expanding the Horizons* was an ambitious vision statement of the improvements which might be possible.

The plans included an interchange between the stations at Hackney Central and Hackney Downs, and four brand new stations:

- Old Oak Common, between Willesden and Acton;
- Chiswick Business Park, between Gunnersbury and Acton;
- King's Cross North, on the site of the Maiden Lane station closed 1917;
- Victoria Docks, on the site of a station closed after bomb damage 1942.

But the North London Line was particularly ill-suited to demonstrate the alleged benefits of private enterprise. There was certainly going to be no money to build new stations. Its trains were worn out – Mike Thirwell of NSE told the London Regional Passengers' Committee,[56] which had been getting a steady supply of complaints over reliability and overcrowding, that the 'electric units are not reliable, averaging only 5,000 miles before failure', while the intensive use didn't leave much time for cleaning and routine maintenance.

Most journeys were short and were contained within travelcard zone two and so they had a low revenue yield. Worse still, the travelcard agreement with London Underground meant that 55 per cent of the revenue went to the Underground anyway.

On 1 April 1994, the privatised world kicked in. The entire infrastructure – track, signalling, bridges, etc – was vested in Railtrack, which operated as a shadow company before being floated on the stock exchange in 1996. The North London Line together with the Watford DC service, and the lines to Northampton, was managed as a shadow franchise called North London Railways under David Watters while private sector bidders were sought.

It didn't look very promising. But there was *some* good news for travellers in this period; from the 31 May 1994 timetable the service frequency was finally to be upped from three trains an hour to four. Two of these ran through to North Woolwich, while two terminated at Stratford. The singling of the track beyond Custom House made it impossible to turn the trains round quickly enough to run four trains an hour on to North Woolwich.

------

56   London Regional Passengers' Committee minutes, 30 March 1994.

Splitting responsibility for operating and infrastructure proved disastrous; it brought lawyers and box-tickers to the fore rather than railway professionals. Railtrack was destined to be a quoted company which aimed to pay high dividends to the shareholders. Its own income consisted of access charges from the train operating companies. But it was reluctant to invest in the infrastructure and relations with the shadow operating companies quickly soured.

Late in 1994, Chris Gibbard, the North London Railways retail manager, told the NLLC: 'We have all been as frustrated as yourselves and all our customers at Railtrack's apparent inability to manage the route'.[57] He must have realised that his comments would find they way into the local press, from where they were duly picked up by the magazine *Modern Railways*, which harboured no illusions about privatisation. For good measure North London Railways added: 'The fault is not ours for the declining standards; we have no control any more over how the track is managed'.

European trains – once again not the needs of north Londoners – were the impetus for what followed.

In October 1991, the government announced that the preferred route for Channel Tunnel trains would be via Stratford and then to a new low-level terminus at King's Cross. Michael Heseltine had argued successfully that this route would help regenerate depressed east London, and the plan was for the trains to run in a new dedicated tunnel all the way.

BR was told to build a reference case and options for this corridor by October 1992. But a second report in early 1993 had a new – and much cheaper – plan which ministers loved. This used St Pancras instead of the expensive King's Cross low level, and would run in tunnel from Stratford to Dalston, and then use two of the four NLL tracks to St Pancras. BR said this option 'need not involve closing the NLL other than for normal track possessions'.[58]

On 22 March the transport secretary, by now John MacGregor, told the Commons that this route would be cheaper and more environmentally friendly and would be the chosen option. Brian Sedgemore, the MP for Hackney South, demanded an assurance that the route from Stratford really would be in tunnel and was not 'a politician's promise, which could be broken as part of a future cost-cutting exercise'. MacGregor gave that assurance, but if Hackney was happy, then next-door Islington definitely wasn't, and another political/transport row erupted.

New campaigns sprung up against the noise and vibration that the work and the new trains would mean; they included: No Channel Tunnel Link Through Islington, whose convenor was Richard Rieser, then a teacher in Hackney, the Barnsbury Rail Action Group, Islington Alert, plus several residents and neighbourhood associations.

---

57   *Hampstead and Highgate Express*, 25 November 1994.
58   British Railways Board Report (Channel Tunnel Rail Link), March 1993.

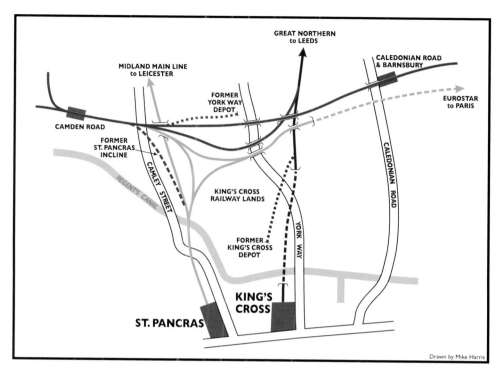

King's Cross – the layout today.

On 29 April 100 people attended a protest meeting at St Jude's Church Hall at Mildmay Grove with many turned away, 130 turned up at the Westbourne Community Centre in Holloway on 18 May, 170 at Harecourt Hall, Canonbury two days later, while 250 crammed into the Union Chapel at Highbury on 1 July for a protest meeting organised by No Channel Tunnel Link Through Islington.

Islington Council stood solidly behind its residents and provided coordinating facilities for community groups fighting the plan. A meeting on 30 September was attended by 17 representatives under the chairmanship of councillor Andrew Bosi.

In June, Chris Smith, an Islington MP, presented three petitions against the plan, from parents, teachers and associates of Canonbury School, the Islington Protection Group and No Channel Tunnel Link Through Islington. The latter complained about 'a possible 150 extra trains every 24 hours destroying the lives of residents and destruction of a green railway corridor which is an important environmental asset for London'. There were another 15 petitions, several from Mildmay Grove and Grosvenor Avenue, roads adjoining the line in the Newington Green area, along with a thousand individual letters.

The Huntingdon Street/Crescent Street/Thornhill Square Union Rail Action Group[59] warned that it would be 6–8 years before the project was completed and during that time 'people will not buy houses in the areas affected, existing owners will not be able to sell. There will be no incentive to improve property and values will fall'.

The local paper, which had greeted the plan as 'Mainline to misery'[60] later quoted extensively from angry residents, reporting that homes were already blighted by the uncertainty.[61] An estate agent warned that potential buyers could spend a lot of money on surveyors and lawyers only to find that building societies would not lend the money. One homeowner near the line had to chop £40,000 – then a huge amount – off the selling price in order to find a buyer, only to find the buyer's building society refused to lend more than half of the selling price, leading to the sale falling through.

The campaign focused on environmental damage – but the impact on North London Line passengers of using two of its tracks could have been enormous. Previously secret documents at Kew reveal that when Union Railways (UR) planned its reference case, its engineers really wanted a complete closure between Highbury and Dalston. They said that although staged construction would allow NLL trains to continue, it would add 1–2 years and £35 million (a 29 per cent increase) to the cost.

The UR reference case, presented to the BRB in November 1992, proposed a shutdown for 'a significant period' with buses replacing trains between Highbury and Dalston. Richmond trains would terminate at Highbury while another shuttle would run between Custom House and Dalston, where a new temporary platform would be needed east of Kingsland station. This would have completely emasculated the service for Hackney residents just when traffic was growing.

However, Union Railways provided options and not recommendations, so a mitigation case provided for two NLL tracks to remain in place during construction.

The impact on NLL passengers was regarded as a very sensitive issue during this process, with many documents marked 'strictly confidential'. A set from Dr John Prideaux, who led for the BRB on the Channel link project, noted: 'There are a lot of highly sensitive issues in this ... if you have any doubt about security of these pieces of paper it would be sensible to destroy them'. Even today it took Freedom of Information Act requests to get access to these files.

Union Railways was under no illusions about the likely reaction to a closure. It regarded the NLL as: 'Highly political, running through several inner London boroughs and serving many low income passengers without access to cars. It is also used by many children travelling to schools in the Hampstead area'.

---

59   Which soon became Barnsbury Rail Action Group.
60   *Islington Gazette*, 25 March 1993.
61   *Islington Gazette*, 25 November 1993.

Hackney Wick: minimum facilities from 1980.

Internally they warned that: 'Several thousand people will suffer a 10 to 20 minute delay, twice a day for two years ... and it quite likely that some of them will be very upset'.

Dalston, which had just acquired a new shopping centre, would be especially hard hit and Union Railways engineers thought that the famous Ridley Road market would have to move: 'It is unlikely that the market could continue in its present form during construction'.

A September 1992 tour of the link route by the entire BRB even avoided visiting north London; a note to NSE managing director John Nelson explained that London was 'off the tour, either because it is too sensitive or because, in the event of a disagreement, the board could have to arbitrate and doesn't want to be seen as compromised'.

Railfreight was relatively content with a planned closure as UR had agreed to pay to electrify the T&H between Gospel Oak and South Tottenham at a cost of £19 million. Freight would then continue down the Lea Valley to Stratford.

However, NSE – which wanted to run more NLL trains - was not happy; it had already rejected the suggestion of providing an end to end service by diverting NLL trains via the T&H and Lea Valley. On 30 November 1992 Geoff Maynard, NSE's business manager for major projects, listed all the drawbacks in a memo to the BRB replying to the Union Railways' reference case:

- Political implications of the two years' closure.
- Extended journey times when traffic on the line was growing.
- Job losses, especially at Ridley Road market.

He concluded that: 'Elsewhere this combination of difficulties would be regarded as a route stopper'. Maynard argued that the baseline reference case should be a tunnel all the way to St Pancras.

The BR board minutes of 3 December 1992 noted the 'implications for traffic currently using the North London Line' and closure seems to have been rejected, for on 24 February 1993, Sir Bob Reid, the BR chairman, was able to write to John MacGregor saying that it had been established that closure of the NLL would not be needed apart from normal track possessions. This assurance was duly confirmed in a Union Railways briefing note, which added that 'some shutdowns, as at present, might be required to undertake specific stages of the work.'[62]

Union Railways' consultation exercise in summer 1993 accepted 'widespread opposition' to using the line. The NLLC also pointed out that dedicating two tracks to European trains would prevent the planned extension of the East London Line to Highbury.

In October, Union Railways finalised its report to the BRB and the ministry. With staged construction on the North London Line a requirement, it turned out that building the disputed section in tunnel would only cost £20 million more, which was not a lot when the total project would cost £2.6 billion, plus, it would save on the cost of upgrade works to the T&H. It would avoid regular weekend closures on the NLL, would be quicker (and therefore cheaper) to build – the staged construction approach would take five years – as well as removing the risks associated with heavy civil engineering work in a confined space next to a working railway.[63]

On 24 January 1994, MacGregor backed down, saying that the route would, after all, be in tunnel, adding: 'The approach to St Pancras has been one of the most contentious issues in London. The surface route along the North London Line corridor would be difficult to construct and environmentally damaging.'[64] But a key lesson was that, once again, effective campaigning, with the active help of the local authority, had won the day. A giant bureaucratic juggernaut really could be stopped if enough people organised themselves and fought hard enough.

Later that year, transport secretary Brian Mawhinney (yet another one!)[65] promised the Conservative Party conference that Eurostar trains would be running on the East Coast Main Line to Leeds and Newcastle within two years. At

---

62   Union Railways, *What will the Union Railway mean for the North London Line*, 1993.
63   British Railways Board report, Union Railways, October 1993.
64   *Independent on Sunday*, 16 January 1994.
65   UK transport secretaries rarely have a chance to understand the issues before the next reshuffle. The 1979–97 Conservative era saw 11 transport secretaries for example.

that time, the Eurostar trains were maintained at a high security depot at North Pole, on the Great Western main line. To reach these from the southern lines leading to the tunnel, the West London Line was electrified on a mixture of DC 750v and AC 25kV in 1993 and an extension to the north of England meant electrifying the North London Line from Willesden Junction to east of Camden Road. Such a plan would also benefit electric freight traffic, which would have another path through north-west London, as well as passenger traffic on the North London Line.

The plan was estimated to cost £16.4 million, and needed a three-month shutdown of Hampstead Tunnel so that the track could be lowered to make space for the overhead wires, and this work was originally pencilled in from September 1994 to January 1995.

But Railtrack got its estimates badly wrong – especially after it found that it had lost £100 million due to a signalmen's dispute. So in October 1994 the work was delayed. The affair was chaotic; *Modern Railways* wrote that Mawhinney had told Sir Robert Horton, the Railtrack boss, "to proceed with the infrastructure works on the basis that the DoT would sort out the funding'.[66] David Watters of North London Railways told Glenda Jackson, the MP for Hampstead, that Whitehall had 'not sufficiently well planned the project' adding that 'major safety issues could have arisen'.[67]

In April 1995 Railtrack got the go-ahead for a new scheme, and planned to shut the line through Hampstead Tunnel from 1 November for 20 weeks. During this time, the North Woolwich trains were diverted to run via Primrose Hill, although the station there remained firmly shut, to terminate at Willesden Low Level, while a Richmond service operated from the High Level platforms. Between Camden Road and Willesden via Hampstead Heath, the passengers were subjected to the delights of the dreaded Rail Replacement bus service.

At the other end of the line, the section from Stratford to North Woolwich was subject to another extended closure, this time between 28 May 1994 and 29 October 1995. This shutdown was to facilitate the extension of the Jubilee Line from Stratford to Canning Town, which runs parallel and just to the west of the North London Line tracks.[68] It meant rail replacement bus services for passengers and lost revenue for the train operator.

---

66 *Modern Railways*, November 1995.
67 *Camden New Journal*, 20 October 1994.
68 The JLE extension to Stratford was a result of the *East London Rail Study*, which was aimed at deciding an eastern terminus for the line, which had originally been mooted to continue to serve the Royal Docks area before diving under the river to Woolwich. Going to Stratford provided a superb interchange for Essex commuters working in Canary Wharf, but the real reason for the diversion was simply that it was cheaper. Had the Woolwich plan materialised, BR Eastern Region would have closed the North London Line east of Custom House, and plans for this were already being made when the legal department advised that they were premature.

The parliamentary agreement between LT and BR protected BR's interests and committed LUL to picking up any net losses which BR could prove. These were reckoned at £13 million a year (£21 million lost revenue minus £8 million from fares on the replacement bus services). But it seems that BR actually saved £130 million from not operating the service. No surprise then that a mooted extension of overhead electrification to this section never took place.

LT paid for rebuilt stations at Canning Town and West Ham; that at Canning Town was re-sited to provide better interchanges with the tube and DLR, while West Ham also provided a more convenient interchange to the District Line. Substantial waterproofing, drainage and pumping work was done on the Connaught Tunnel under the channel between the Victoria and Albert Docks which was prone to flooding. Now that the line was electrified on the third rail system any flooding here would close the service, and the steam age option of using the high-level route over a swing bridge belonging to the Port of London Authority Railways was no longer available as the track had been removed years before. This work was paid for by the London Docklands Development Corporation.

Fixing all this outdated infrastructure was long overdue, but the regular weekend and occasional extended closures needed to do this were a prime cause of the North London Line's poor reputation in the 1990s. The first long closure was actually in the 1980s, and followed a subsidence-induced collapse in Hampstead Tunnel leading to the line being closed from 2 December 1984 to 15 April 1985 with repairs costing £1.3 million, but the pace picked up dramatically in the 1990s.

Some (very little) sympathy might possibly be extended to Railtrack. Although it was to become one of the most despised companies in British corporate history, it was hardly its fault that successive governments had failed to give BR the money to invest in boring, unspectacular infrastructure through the 1970s and 1980s. When Railtrack did need blockages, it made engineering sense to give the contractors complete possession, and usually meant that the work could be achieved more quickly. But replacement bus services provided a poor alternative.

The Camden Road to Willesden service should have resumed in March 1996. But Railtrack's engineers had found more problems; the viaduct section between Gospel Oak and Camden Road was in a poor state after decades of neglect and it made sense to do the repairs there and then rather than restore service only to demand another blockage in the future. And so the blockage was extended again, replacement bus services continued and services did not resume until 29 September.

What was essentially a brand new railway required the engineers laying 78 miles of cable, adjusting the track below 17 overbridges, and relaying 7 miles of track with the old conductor rails removed. The final cost was over £60 million. By extending the AC catenary to Acton, the 313 units could use

Southbound at Acton Wells Junction in NSE days.

DC power from North Woolwich to Hackney Wick, AC power from there to Dalston, where the pantograph to collect current from the overhead wires was lowered. They would then switch to DC current for the stretch to Camden Road where the pantograph was again raised to take AC current until Acton Central, and from there the trains ran on DC current into Richmond.

The electrification did improve passenger services as the 313 stock ran noticeably better on new AC wires than on the old DC conductor rails. Hampstead Heath even got new wooden platform canopies in the traditional style!

The coming of the fast link to St Pancras enabled Eurostar trains to pass on to the North London Line by modifying the existing spur from Camden Road to the Great Northern line to include a link on to Eurostar tracks. But the main objective of the project was a failure; Eurostar trains never have run to Leeds or Newcastle. Without a dedicated high-speed track in the UK, air travel was well ahead on time and, with the coming of low-cost airlines, on cost too.

More misery was to follow for passengers as the trains resumed on the old 20-minute frequency, rather than the improved 15-minute one. North London Railways told passengers that traffic had fallen during the long closure (funny, that) and so the enhanced service could not be justified. It promised to restore the full service when traffic picked up again, but it wasn't until September 1997 that a 15-minute headway was restored and then only between Stratford and Camden Road. Not until January 1999 did the entire line have a 15-minute service.

By this time the North London was a fully privatised railway. On 7 February 1997 the North London Railways franchise was sold to National Express, a publicly-quoted coach operator whose roots were with the former state-owned National Bus Company. National Express beat off Connex, which was destined to be an unloved train operator south of the river, and Great Western. National Express renamed its network Silverlink. The franchise was due to run until 15 October 2006.

Meanwhile, the Labour government which took office in 1997 delivered on one of its promises. It created the post of a directly elected mayor heading a new Greater London Assembly – and Ken Livingstone returned to power as an independent candidate in May 2000. A year later his Transport Strategy included the following objectives:

1. A high frequency turn-up-and-go-service of four trains per hour;
2. More reliable and less crowded services;
3. A more secure passenger environment;
4. Integrated ticketing, especially the acceptance of Oyster cards on the National Rail network;
5. Development of an orbital railway for London, and;
6. Development of bypass routes to avoid freight passing through London when it was destined for the Midlands and the North.

Among the team who wrote the crucial chapter on national rail, which argued for a massive investment in orbital transport, was John Sanderson, the ex-NLLC secretary who had worked as a transport planner for both Islington and Enfield councils. It was Sanderson who got the crucial backing for the chapter from Redmond O'Neill, Livingstone's deputy chief of staff, and today he says 'I personally regard my best achievement in 30 years in transport planning as getting the orbitrail concept seeded into that chapter. Once there as a mayoral objective, TfL or more specifically London Rail (who I subsequently worked for), took it on board. As a new independent directorate in TfL it gave them something they could achieve and make their mark with.'

Achieving all this meant Livingstone needed control and that meant getting government support. The new government had not initially regarded public transport as a priority, but the Hatfield rail disaster of October 2000 forced the issue and was the beginning of the end for Railtrack. Immediate major repairs were ordered at a cost of £580 million and Railtrack imposed panicky emergency speed restrictions which brought the railways to a virtual standstill. Whitehall opinion was outraged by the spiralling cost of the West Coast Main Line modernisation plan and the fact that Railtrack used government funding to pay shareholders a £137 million dividend in May 2001. Trade and industry secretary Stephen Byers forced it into administration and from the ashes rose Network Rail, a not-for-profit company which would manage infrastructure going forward.

John Sanderson.

In January 2004, a thorough review of Britain's railways was announced, and two months later, Livingstone's transport chief, the US-born Bob Kiley, proposed the setting up of a London Regional Rail Authority to take control of all passenger traffic in the capital, including the ex-BR suburban commuter lines. Under this proposal, Transport for London (TfL) would take the risk on revenue, rolling stock contracts and upgrading works, so reducing franchise costs and ending compensation payments to train operators. More frequent services, it was argued, could lead to a five per cent increase in capacity, and cut over-crowding and journey times within two years. The Oyster card would be extended to rail services, while tube-style zonal ticketing would simplify things for travellers, who could pay between £1.70 and £3.70 for a zone three to zone one journey on national rail depending on location. Stations would be upgraded and made more secure.

By then, London was bidding to host the 2012 Olympics. But in its initial assessment of London's bid, the International Olympic Committee (IOC) slammed London's antiquated transport infrastructure, saying 'Rail public transport is often obsolete and considerable investments must be made to upgrade the existing system in terms of capacity and safety'.

Poor transport meant London's bid was ranked lower than those from Paris and Madrid, and the bid would go no further unless something was very publicly seen to be done about it.

There was one hint that progress might be possible. It affected the related issue of extending London Transport's East London Line trains over the disused viaduct south of Dalston (see next chapter). The project had been stalled and TfL argued that it should take responsibility for building the line, and by May *New Civil Engineer* had reported that 'Ministers are considering whether the project should be funded through central government or Ken Livingstone's Transport for London'. But TfL wasn't optimistic – the June 2004 TfL board papers glumly noted that 'government has indicated that it is unlikely to be in a position to fund the full East London Line scheme and it has concerns about the proposed funding process using Design Build Finance Transfer'.[69]

A July 2004 White Paper on rail transport duly followed, containing the best news possible for the bruised and battered passengers on the North London.[70] The government agreed to more powers for the mayor and committed itself to working with Livingstone's team to rationalise fare structures and ticketing technology across different types of public transport. Crucially, the government would 'explore urgently options for giving an increased role to the mayor on discrete services that lie entirely, or almost entirely, within the GLA boundary'.

---

69   The variant of the PFI under consideration to pay for ELLE.
70   White Paper – *The Future of Rail*, cmd 6233.

The same month, the government agreed a five-year financial settlement to TfL of £10 billion, made up of £2.7 billion in direct government grant, the right to 'prudentially borrow' up to £3.3 billion plus £4 billion of PPP expenditure for the controversial privatisation of the tube infrastructure. All this covered several schemes that TfL was paying for and had offered to the IOC in its contribution to the Olympics bid – including the East London Line Extension.[71]

On 6 November 2004 it was announced that ELLE, which was likely to have been developed as a main line project, probably as part of the Southern franchise, would be transferred from the Strategic Rail Authority, where it had mouldered, to TfL who would definitely build it.

All this was an astonishing turnaround in Whitehall, and was enshrined in the 2005 Railways Act. The Labour Party hierarchy disliked and distrusted Livingstone and had tried hard to block his election as mayor in 2000. Agreeing to Livingstone's proposals was a far-sighted act therefore – and one which seemed to have come as a surprise to Livingstone himself.[72]

In February 2006, the transport department delivered. It agreed that the Silverlink franchise would be split in two, with the lines to Northampton and Rugby being transferred to a new London Midland franchise under a new privatised entity, while the North London Line and the Watford DC service would be given to Transport for London. The combined Silverlink franchise was extended until November 2007 to allow for the transition.

Ironically, the structure introduced by privatisation helped the handover of control. When it was suggested that London Transport take over the line in the 1960s, the idea was rejected because of the large amount of freight traffic. But now, with infrastructure and operations split off, it was possible to hand over operational control of services, and at long last the key decisions on a London rail service would be taken by elected politicians accountable to Londoners.

When the London Assembly looked at the North London Line in 2006 it documented in detail the mess that it would shortly inherit. It reported that passengers 'expressed real discontent about the reliability and frequency of the trains, unattractive stations with poor provision for passengers, grubby and ageing rolling stock, and unsatisfactory ticketing arrangements'. The GLA report was titled *London's Forgotten Railway* and featured a quote from one passenger who called the line 'Shabby, unreliable, unsafe, overcrowded'.

It was a decade since 19-year-old Alison Day had been dragged from a train at Hackney Wick and raped and murdered by two men who had committed a string of other attacks, yet staffing remained a central issue; the report went on: 'Stations are often unstaffed, which makes many passengers feel unsafe'.

---

71 Plus the DLR extensions to London City Airport and Woolwich Arsenal, capacity enhancement on the DLR and bus transit schemes.

72 In his autobiography *You Can't Say That* he recalls that he was on holiday in France at the time and when his negotiator gave him the news by phone, he says he would have fallen into the pool had he not been sitting down.

LOND**ON** ASSEMBLY   Transport Committee

London's Forgotten Railway
The Transport Committee's review of the North London Railway
March 2006

The Greater London
Assembly's damning look at
the line before the TfL
takeover.

At this time, the London *Evening Standard* had been running a campaign to
pressure train-operating companies into keeping stations staffed throughout
opening hours after Thomas Ap Rhys-Price was murdered shortly after leaving
the unstaffed Kensal Green station (on the Watford DC line) on 12 January
2006. The killers – later caught and jailed – had also visited the station that
same night, a short time before the murder, and mugged a man on the
platform.

There had been other, less publicised attacks too – in early 1997 two women
were the subject of a terrifying assault at Caledonian Road where they were
robbed, forced across the live electric tracks to a remote area where they were
stripped and indecently assaulted. A Silverlink project to assess the need for
CCTV at all stations had still not started six months later.[73]

One female member of the North London Line Committee had been attacked
and robbed on the line at night, but refused to stop using it on the grounds that
if everyone did that then trains would simply be withdrawn.

---

73   *Highbury and Islington Express*, 21 November 1997.

Unstaffing of stations made it much less likely that travellers – particularly women – would use the service at night. It certainly saved money on staff costs – but also directly hit revenue as people did not use the service. In any case, fare collection was erratic. Said the GLA: 'The North London Railway has built up a reputation as the "free railway" in recent years'. There were very few of the automatic entrance gates which were deployed on LT lines. Single journey passengers had to buy tickets on the train from a conductor, if there was one. But during peak hours, trains were so overcrowded that conductors could not move along the train! An exercise had shown that 13 per cent of passengers had not bought a ticket. Imposing a £20 penalty fare from January 2006 cut this figure to six per cent.

TfL hired design consultants to report on the heritage features of the line. They were entirely unimpressed by the 1960s' station buildings. Of Canonbury they said: 'It is dark, mean, and poorly designed with little surveillance from the ticket office, cramped and utterly devoid of architectural merit'. Moving on to Hampstead Heath they noted: 'It is a dark, mean and unwelcoming facility more akin to a public convenience' while Finchley Road was 'similarly cramped and uninviting'.

The Strategic Rail Authority's autumn 2000 National Passenger Survey[74] showed how dire things were, or more correctly, how dire passengers thought they were. On every reasonable measure Silverlink had the worst rating of all the privatised companies.

Table seven – Silverlink and passenger satisfaction – 2000

Quality measure	% of Silverlink passengers either dissatisfied or very dissatisfied	Silverlink ranking out of 25 train operating companies
Punctuality/reliability	41	Worst
Overall opinion of journey	26	Worst
Frequency	25	Worst
Value for money	47	Worst
Information about train times/platforms	25	Worst
Upkeep or repair of train	23	Joint eighth worst
Length of journey time	18	Worst
Amount of seats/ standing space	30	Joint worst
Connections	18	Second worst
Comfort of seats	25	Second worst
Station ticket buying facilities	23	Third worst
Passenger capacity	20	Joint third worst

---

74   Strategic Rail Authority – *On Track, Rail Performance Trends, April–October 2000.*

It is noticeable that it had the worst rating for length of journey – a remarkable failure given the short journey lengths. This has to be a reflection of how passengers saw the overall experience. These figures were for the entre Silverlink franchise including the lines to Northampton. There is a suspicion that if the North London Line were split out the feedback would have been even worse.

By June 2001, the SRA began to track complaints handling too. Silverlink was still the third worst offender in the South East region, and it generated more complaints than operators carrying far more passengers such as South West Trains, West Anglia Great Northern and the two Connex franchises. The SRA also found that Silverlink replied to only 31 per cent of its complaints within the target time, putting it in 22nd place out of 25 operators.

However campaigners involved with the line often turn out to have considerable sympathy for Silverlink. Jonathan Roberts says they came to the franchise with 'great ambitions' including a major hub at Willesden Junction but were thwarted by the terms of the franchise contract, while Peter Staveley, who we will meet shortly, says 'They never had any money to do anything – it was set up as a minimum cost franchise'. The franchise in fact laid down that public subsidy would fall from £54 million in 1996/97 to just £36 million two years later – a guarantee of a worse service to come.

Silverlink had certainly tried to improve the service. With the help of the SRA, it had put on extra trains in May 2004. In January 2005 TfL had paid for additional evening services – the so-called PiXC busters (for Passengers In eXcess of Capacity, one of the many useful acronyms that privatisation introduced to the railways), and some of these had been extended to Clapham Junction, providing the first Stratford – Willesden – Clapham service. But Silverlink warned that each time it had introduced PiXC busters over the past five years, the traffic had simply increased to fill them. Silverlink managers thought there was 'substantial suppressed demand and that traffic growth is far higher than underlying economic and development changes would suggest'.[75]

By 2006 Silverlink claimed that reliability had improved since December 2004, and some of those who spoke to the GLA Committee agreed. In early 2004, more than a quarter of North London trains were more than five minutes late. This figure had been reduced to one in ten by the end of 2004. But in 2005, it rose again to 15 per cent. Silverlink attributed this to two specific problems: the impact of the 7/7 bombings and a hole in the track at Dalston.

Train reliability is measured by the Public Performance Measure (PPM) which monitors the percentage of trains arriving at their destination within five minutes of the booked time. It is clear that Silverlink performance was improving. For most of the early 21st century its PPM was hovering around the 80 per cent mark, hitting a low of 77 per cent in the third quarter of 2003–04. But it had risen to 90 per cent in the first quarter of 2005–2006

---

75   *London Lines* response to Network Rail Cross-London traffic RUS, February 2006.

Table eight – Silverlink PPM improvements 2001–2006

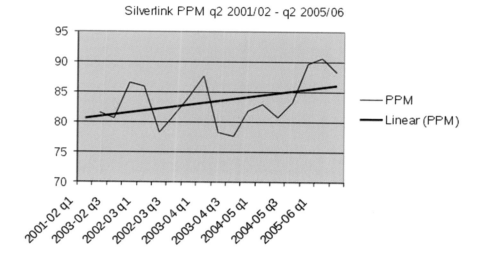

Silverlink PPM q2 2001/02 - q2 2005/06

Legend: —— PPM   —— Linear (PPM)

x-axis labels: 2001-02 q1, 2003-02 q3, 2002-03 q1, 2002-03 q3, 2003-04 q1, 2003-04 q3, 2004-05 q1, 2004-05 q3, 2005-06 q1

y-axis: 70, 75, 80, 85, 90, 95

Camden Road's listed exterior shown in BR days.

The general improvement was put down to the removal – after discussions with Network Rail – of 14 speed restrictions along the line, improved track maintenance, including the use of an ultrasonic test train to find minor rail cracks, and a timetable readjustment which meant that, from 2005, it more accurately reflected factors such as dwell time at stations.

One significant barrier to reliability turned out to be the dead section between Bollo Lane Junction and Gunnersbury. This amounted to around seven carriages and so North London trains needed to coast over this gap without a power supply. If the train ran out of momentum then there was no power to get the train moving again and it had to wait until it could be pushed by another train. There were about three incidents of this type a year.

London's Forgotten Railway supported Silverlink's views on suppressed demand: 'The delays experienced by passengers week on week, with indeterminate waits at dirty, unsafe and poorly maintained stations must deter many. A smart, clean, reliable and frequent service may well turn out to trigger unprecedented levels of demand.'

Given the unreliable service, poor communication was a major complaint. If a train was running late did you wait for it? If delay turned into cancellation, did you give it up and walk or take the bus (even if there was one for your journey) as the next train would be impossibly full? You had no information on which to base your decision.

The explanation deserves to be printed in full as it captures the foolishness of privatising a key national asset and then doing so in the most foolish way possible:

'An auto-announcer system, which was owned by Network Rail and leased by Silverlink, was used. When the train passed a reporting spot the information on all the stations was updated, however if a train broke down once it had passed a reporting spot the information would not be updated. Updates were made after the train driver had contacted the Network Rail signaller. In addition the system was geared towards signalling and not towards the customer. The system was centralised so it could not be turned off and local announcements had to be typed in or pre-recorded announcements downloaded. This was not the role of station staff however who were employed to be in control of the ticket office and not to deal with announcements. On-board passengers had to rely on conductors to give on-board announcements. Conductors therefore needed pagers and mobiles. Network Rail would only replace like with like so a new system would need investment by a third party such as TfL.'

One of the few attempts to run medium distance services over the North London Line was already over. In May 2000 Anglia Railways had started a service between Basingstoke and Ipswich. This was supported with funding from the Strategic Rail Authority through its Rail Passenger Partnership fund, which was designed to give initial support to rail passenger schemes which may be slow to start.

The service was called London Crosslink and ran up to five times a day. Trains called only at Stratford, Highbury, Camden Road, West Hampstead and Willesden on the North London Line. Capacity constraints limited the number which could be run, and the service pattern was uneven – so trains only stopped at Camden Road at weekends.

The service was not a success and ended on 11 September 2002 after the SRA withdrew financial support. TfL were not sad to see it go; Ian Brown told the Rail Transport Advisory Panel: 'A service which attracted customers in single figures clearly could not be sustained. In addition it consumed capacity on a core orbital route which could be put to better use'.

TfL needed a good working relationship with local councils along the route, and so in June 2005 it sponsored the setting up of the North Orbital Rail Partnership (NORP) which eventually covered 16 boroughs. Its secretary was Peter Staveley, a transport consultant and former BR traffic planner who was then working for Brent Council.

He recalls: 'The initiative came from TfL, who called a meeting. They wanted boroughs to be able to speak with one voice, and be able to provide a lobbying group. They wanted answers from us and were very open in their approach.'

Amid North Woolwich tower blocks – the footbridge to Factory Road has now been demolished.

NORP was responsible for coordinating the improvement of access to stations on the line together with TfL London Rail and TfL Borough Partnerships, who provided some (but not all) of the funding. The aim was to complement TfL's improvement of station infrastructure and train services with enhanced and safer access for passengers from areas surrounding the stations.

A critical achievement was to work with the signal engineers at Network Rail to ensure that the signal layout would allow six-car trains to be run if needed in the future and if funding existed for it. Staveley says: 'It can easily cost £1 million to move two signals and we were really worried about being stuck with four-car trains for the next 40 years'.[76]

TfL, meanwhile, was finalising the service pattern it wanted. Suggestions that ELLE could be extended to Finsbury Park or Willesden Low Level via Queen's Park and Primrose Hill, which appeared in the Mayor's Transport Strategy in 2001, had vanished by 2005.

But TfL definitely wanted:

- Four trains per hour Stratford – Richmond
- Four trains per hour Stratford – Queen's Park via Primrose Hill, a plan linked to extending Bakerloo Line trains to Watford
- Four trains per hour Barking – Clapham Junction via Gospel Oak and Willesden High Level, all predicated on electrifying Gospel Oak – Barking

However, TfL thought that with more trains running, three-car trains would remain sufficient until 2016.

In November 2005, Network Rail published its Route Utilisation Strategy (RUS) for all cross-London services. Producing a complete set of RUS for the entire network was an obligation inherited from the old Strategic Rail Authority. The declared aim was to 'seek to balance supply and demand and set out our longer term vision for improvements across the network'. A RUS would consider existing capacity, infrastructure and train operations, forecast future demand and provide recommendations on how this could be managed.

The Cross-London RUS was finalised in August 2006 after consultation with all stakeholders, and the consultation replies were all published too. It was an impressive and balanced 77-page report, made publicly available for all to see and comment upon.

Network Rail's proposals were set against the forecast of continued population growth, with London expected to grow over the next 15 years by another 810,000 people – more than the entire population of Frankfurt or Glasgow. As a result, underlying passenger demand was forecast to grow by 17 per cent by 2017.

---

76   NORP was wound up in 2011 when TfL changed the basis of its funded partnerships.

Freight on the North London Line: Freightliner class 66 at Camden Road.

But freight traffic was also rising – international traffic from the Channel Tunnel was up 19 per cent from 2002 to 2003, and Network Rail reckoned that around 24 additional daily freight paths would be needed each way on the North London Line and around 10 on the Gospel Oak to Barking route by 2014, mainly because of growth in deep sea container traffic.

Environmentally this was a good thing. Freightliner said that rail's share of deep sea container traffic had risen from 17 per cent in 1996 to 25 per cent in 2006 – traffic which would otherwise have clogged up the roads and added to pollution in so doing. But the RUS said that this expected growth 'cannot be met within the current freight services in the working timetable'. And this traffic had to go over the North London Line from Stratford before passing via Primrose Hill on to the West Coast Main Line; this was the *only* rail route from the Thames-side and east coast ports which could accommodate the latest 9½ft high containers (the so-called W10 loading gauge) bound for the Midlands and north. The AC electrification from Stratford to Camden in 1986 for freight was partly designed to encourage operators to use this route, but since then, in a shortsighted attempt to save money on bridge replacement costs and viaduct improvements, the Barking to Gospel Oak route had not been improved. It suffered from speed limits over the decaying viaduct sections through Leyton and Wanstead and long stretches between signal boxes which limited the number of trains which could operate. It couldn't handle the W10 (or even the smaller W9) type containers, and was still not electrified, meaning that freight trains required expensive changes of traction at both ends. Electrification of this line was not listed as an option in the RUS – to the great annoyance of the Barking – Gospel Oak Line User Group. When the North London Line was converted to AC in 1996 another opportunity had been lost to enable Hampstead Tunnel to take W10 size wagons.

All this was the old, old issue: the balance between passengers and freight for the fixed number of paths which the infrastructure would allow to be crammed into the timetable. (Technically a train path is the infrastructure capacity needed to run a train between two places over a given time-period. So better signalling, etc = more paths.)

Fundamentally this is a sub-text which has occurred regularly throughout this study – the extent to which communities in north London had first claim on what they considered to be their railway.

When the draft RUS went to consultation, the London Lines Consortium, which included Silverlink, talked darkly of 'concern that best use is not made of existing pathways'. It asked to see 'further details of the volume of freight traffic moved compared to the potential capacity allocated'.

The working timetable did allow paths for freight trains which were never used – quite a lot of them in fact. At Camden Road for example, the average take-up of paths was only 65 per cent and the maximum was 85 per cent. But it didn't follow that these 'spare' paths could be used for a better passenger service:

- There were duplicates – multiple paths for the same train to allow for diversions when lines were closed for engineering work.
- Some paths were required for seasonal traffic.
- Customers' trains may actually not run due to interruptions to processes (quarries for example) or end-user demand such as bad weather on construction sites.
- End customers' needs can change more quickly than the timetable production cycle can amend paths, so trains were running to different short term plans from those in the timetable.

While it was to everyone's advantage that heavy freight moved by rail and not by road, Network Rail acknowledged that north Londoners had to be given more consideration: 'Historically, these lines have been seen as strategic freight routes, but fast rising passenger demand is forcing the industry to review this status'.

It reckoned that if growth continued the way it had, and nothing was done about it, by 2016, westbound peak hour trains would be over their capacity all the way from Stratford to Caledonian Road. In plain speaking, a significant number of commuters simply would not be able to insert themselves into the travelling sardine can – they just wouldn't fit. And perhaps they would consider themselves the lucky ones compared with those who did manage to get on board. Seats, meanwhile, wouldn't be available on a westbound train until it had passed Hampstead Heath. Clearly this was unacceptable.

Official figures might even have understated the situation. TfL told local councils in the North London Line area that average passenger growth would be 1.32 per cent a year based on growth since 2001. Hackney wasn't convinced. Roger Blake, a Hackney Council transport planner, had carried out his own survey at Hackney Wick between 2004 and 2005 and found that passenger growth was six per cent higher than what TfL had estimated. Based on this research, Hackney teamed up with Islington and Camden councils to carry out a more detailed survey of 10 stations[77] and together they concluded that passenger growth was 6.6 per cent higher each year than the official figures.

How come? Hackney concluded that:

- Network Rail and TfL may have used data that was based on too narrow a time band (one hour), and may under-record ridership on the North London Line.
- Silverlink's 5–10 per cent estimates for fare evasion were too low.

Hackney reported all this back to Network Rail as part of the RUS feedback, saying that passenger growth on the line would be higher than the TfL forecasts, meaning that line upgrades should support six-coach trains in 'the very near future'.

The RUS listed four options to solve the passenger crisis on the North London Line:

- Reconfigure the internal seating within the 313 class trains to provide more standing space.
- Run extra peak hour trains – more PiXC busters. This had helped in the past, but more capacity was required than could be met by this alone.
- Increase the trains from three coaches to four or six. Four cars were reckoned to be enough over the RUS period, and the total cost of doing this would be between £48 and £109 million.
- Run trains every 15 minutes Stratford to Richmond and every 15 minutes Stratford to Queen's Park via Primrose Hill. This would mean eight trains per hour between Camden and Stratford. The Barking to Gospel Oak service would then be extended to Clapham Junction.

All this was found to be feasible and could be fitted in among the freight paths, but it would need infrastructure improvements.

While discussion of options continued, TfL provided its passengers with a token of good faith on 2 January 2008, when it changed the travelcard zone boundaries so that Hampstead Heath moved from zone three to zone two, while Willesden Junction, previously in zone three, moved to the zone two/three boundary. The effect was to make some journeys cheaper, and to reverse the pre-privatisation move, naturally retained by Silverlink, which put Hampstead Heath in zone three, even though it is actually nearer to Charing Cross than Hampstead tube station, which was in zone two.

But before we look at what TfL did when it won control, we need to go back in time somewhat to look at the on-off plans for restoring services over the disused North London Line section south of Dalston.

---

77   They were Hackney Wick to West Hampstead inclusive. Hackney remains convinced that official figures continue to understate passenger usage, not just on the North London Line but elsewhere in the capital too.

1987–2004:
'THE EAST LONDON CONNECTION'

In which we look at the story of the East London Line Extension over the old Broad Street viaduct – or how it took almost 25 years of political arguments and false starts to build a few miles of railway.

The genesis of what was to become the reborn North London Line City link came in 1985, when BR was attempting to realise its their investment in the Bishopsgate Goods Yard. This had lain derelict since the spectacular fire of 5 December 1964 which killed two people and cost – according to the insurers' estimate – £5 million, a huge sum for the time.

The site was made up of 10 acres – equivalent to 20 football pitches. It was tantalisingly close to a City of London which was beginning to expand out of its traditional boundaries – and almost within sight of the Broadgate development which had rung the original death knell for the Broad Street link only a year or two previously.

Legal challenges defeated and work can now start.

The reborn City link would have to involve some kind of extension of the East London Line: that maroon bit of the tube map which seemed to go from nowhere to nowhere, ending in a curious stub terminating at Shoreditch, where a symbol on the map told you that the station was open only at peak hours. The forgotten East London Line certainly had character – Wapping station's narrow platforms were open at their north end in a deep cutting where ferns grew from the retaining walls and water rolled down; at the south end the waiting passenger could peer into the stygian mystery of Marc Brunel's Thames Tunnel. By 1985, traffic was beginning to rise again due to the redevelopment of the Wapping area, but it was far below its 1950s' heyday. While the history of the East London Line itself is out of the scope of this study, its extension to Dalston is fairly and squarely part of North London Line history.

LT had not quite given up on its attempts to get the East London Line into Liverpool Street and with the demise of plans to reopen the direct link west of Shoreditch LT into Liverpool Street, any moves in that direction had to involve the Bishopsgate site, which, sooner or later, would be sold for office development.

Bishopsgate Goods Yard before the fire – looking south towards the City.

In 1985 and 1986, a joint LT/BR working party considered the case for converting some lightly used sections of line in the capital to light rail. Most of the schemes considered were in outer London, but it was suggested that the East London could be converted to light rail, and extended from Whitechapel to Liverpool Street. It would run via Bishopsgate Goods, where a new station would be built, over a new bridge across Shoreditch High Street before turning down into Liverpool Street over the remains of the North London viaduct. Almost as an afterthought it was added that this could be extended to Dalston.[78] This suggestion made its way into *Light Rail for London*, published in 1986, which was the blueprint for what became the Croydon tramlink.

The proposal got a lukewarm reception from parts of the British Rail Property Board (BRPB). Its business focus was on property development, not public transport, and it had already hired Savills, a major property consultant, to value the site. BRPB was already concerned that plans to increase the main line tracks into Liverpool Street from six to eight – to provide passengers with a better service – would hurt the sale value. Savills reckoned that as a whole the site was worth £3.75 million, but with 'reservations' for other uses, it would fall to between £0.8 million and £1.6 million.

The local councils covering Bishopsgate, Tower Hamlets and Hackney, were extremely keen on an extension to Dalston to boost their urban regeneration plans, and reservations for it would certainly be required. Hackney would subsequently use planning law (a so-called Section 106 agreement) to make development conditional on the extension being built. But C J Smith, the BRPB estates and survey manager, wrote on 7 May 1986: 'What has not been tested is how adamant Tower Hamlets would be about the East London Line if it were demonstrated that the reservation would blight the whole site'. In 1988, Pat Scutt at BRPB described an extension to Dalston as a 'threat' which would divide Bishopsgate from other developments to the south.

LUL set up an East London Extension Steering Group in spring 1987. But the extension to Dalston was by no means a certainty; in September that year, the third meeting heard that 'general impressions by the consultants are not that favourable to the extension' unless major development took place in the Shoreditch area. As late as September 1988, it seemed that any extension would need to be a light rail equivalent of the Docklands Light Railway as the gradient needed to cross the Great Eastern main line was estimated at 1 in 19, too steep for normal trains. Discussions had taken place with the city councils in both Dortmund and Frankfurt, which had old trams which could be bought. But there clearly remained some doubt about the viability of the entire project because the 9 September steering committee meeting noted that it was decided 'not to abandon the northern extension at this stage'.

---

78   Another scheme considered for light rail was the Stratford to North Woolwich section of the North London Line, which had only just been electrified.

Meanwhile, BRPB was looking for a developer for the Bishopsgate site. By early 1989, London and Edinburgh Trust (LET), a leading property firm, and the one which had handled the nearby Spitalfields Market redevelopment, had emerged as the lead developer. It proposed a classic Big City scheme for the site, with 1.5 million square feet of office space including a 20-storey tower block. In response to calls for community involvement from the Tower Hamlets Environment Trust, LET embarked, to the apparent dismay of BRPB, on a public consultation scheme. Other interested developers steered well clear of this public involvement, partly because each developer had an obligation to keep its proposals secret. BR even warned LET that 'the publicity could disqualify their scheme'. Even so, in April 1989, what one observer called 'the façade of community involvement'[79] helped LET beat four other firms to become the preferred developer of the site.

On 7 September, the LT board backed the principle of extending the line, and the extension appeared as one of the several railway options considered in the East London Assessment Study, one of four such studies, commissioned by Nick Ridley to take a complete look at transport across the London boroughs.

It recommended – in November 1989 – that the scheme proceed, estimating that there would be 2,600 passengers per hour each way between Dalston and Whitechapel. However the consultants from Ove Arup who were responsible for the report were less convinced by the northern extension onto Highbury, calculating that it would carry less than 500 passengers per hour adding that 'there seems little justification for this.' It proposed instead to build an interchange with the North London Line at a combined Dalston station. The report added that local redevelopment could be generated at Dalston and to a lesser degree at Hackney caused by the areas' greater attractiveness to higher income groups. It also thought that the extension could not be justified south of Surrey Docks.

More controversially, the assessment studies also recommended a new bout of road building to ease congestion in the capital, and for a while it looked as though the ghost of the 1960s motorways could walk (drive?) again. But in March 1990, to jubilation all across the capital, Cecil Parkinson, the transport minister, ruled out the new road building proposals contained in the studies.

But none of this meant that ELLE – the East London Line Extension – would be built. London Transport wanted it, the boroughs involved wanted it. But who was going to pay for it?

The politics of transport investment in this period were illustrated in the *East London Rail Study*, produced by Halcrow Fox, an engineering consulting firm, to define the best option for extending the Jubilee Line into Docklands. It made it clear that the government expected that major transport schemes should be paid for by those who benefited from them, whether passengers, property

---

79 Graham Towers, *Building democracy: community architecture in the Inner Cities.*

developers or landowners. Only exceptionally would the government expect to support public transport projects because there were benefits to non-users – in terms of reduced traffic congestion for example.

This ideologically based approach had the side-effect of placing property developers in a strong position vis-à-vis cash strapped local authorities. There was a clear trade off: you get the transport link you need to regenerate your area if I get the planning permission. And in reality, the deal seemed even more skewed in favour of developers – Olympia and York, the developers of Canary Wharf, paid £400 million towards the Jubilee Line Extension, which massively benefited their investment. The huge cost overruns on this project meant that this contribution eventually amounted to around only five per cent of the cost, even though the idea was that the developers would pay a large part of the bill.

Early 1990 saw agitation within LT to pin LET down. They had offered a 'substantial contribution' to the cost of the line, and on 14 March the finance committee heard that: 'Negotiations should commence with LET to establish the value of their substantial contribution'. But what LET really wanted was an interchange on the Central Line, which passes directly below the site. On 14 March LUL's development director told the LUL board: 'LET have insisted on the inclusion of a Central Line station and have informally indicated that they would be prepared to meet the full cost'. This was put at £42 million. Central Line management was said to be in favour of the plan although it would add 1.1 minutes to journey times.

Eventually LET came up with a figure for their 'substantial contribution' – £50 million. It would pay this when scheme started to be implemented – which was planned for March 1992. The total project cost was put at £177 million, a figure independently verified by the Halcrow Fox consultancy.

Time was running out though. LT planned to deposit a bill in November and the extensions were critical to LET winning planning permission from Tower Hamlets and Hackney. On 20 July, the planning director told the board that LET's 'current offer would be insufficient to cover the cost' of the Central Line platforms at Bishopsgate, adding that it was now 'unrealistic' to aim for a November deadline to deposit the bill.

On 20 September, the development director stressed again the relative ease of the project. He told the board: 'The extensions do not pose major civil engineering problems; could run largely over BR or derelict land, do not present major property acquisition, demolition nor environmental issues and should not encounter major opposition'. But on 21 November, Cecil Parkinson announced postponement. He told the Commons that despite LET's £50 million contribution: 'The project as a whole would still require substantial public funding. Given the public expenditure constraints within which it must operate, London Transport has concluded that it has other more pressing priorities at present and has therefore decided, with my agreement, not to seek leave to deposit the necessary private bill in this session of Parliament'.

Some mystery remains over why LT did not pursue its bill. Michael Schabas, who was then the transport lead for Olympia and York at Canary Wharf, said that ELLE was probably overshadowed by more prestigious projects such as the Jubilee Line Extension and Crossrail, even though ELLE had 'a benefit/cost ratio far superior to those of the other schemes which did proceed, and a scheme cost an order of magnitude smaller'.

But internally, LT's ELLE steering group put the blame squarely on Parkinson. The minutes of the 10 December meeting noted bitterly that: 'The project had reached a position where a bill deposit in the November 1990 session would have been possible *if the secretary of state's consent had been forthcoming* (author's italics). A draft book of references, environmental impact study and department of transport submission had been prepared. The parliamentary plans had been produced ... public consultation was well advanced.'

It was clear that a proper ELLE lobby group totally independent of LT was needed. The abolition of the GLC left the capital with no strategic transport authority. London Underground was, through the unelected London Regional Transport quango, directly responsible to Whitehall and could hardly lobby against it.

The result was the East London Line Group (ELLG), which coalesced during 1990, and received a formal stimulus when Roger Freeman, visiting Bishopsgate as transport minister in September 1991, implied to officials from Hackney and Southwark councils that 'if you want this railway you'll need to lobby for it'.

The group's supporters represented everyone who stood to gain:

- Local councils – initially Hackney, Islington, Tower Hamlets, Lewisham and Southwark.
- Property developers – Grand Metropolitan (who owned the former Truman's brewery site on Brick Lane), London and Edinburgh Trust, and the British Rail Property Board.
- Urban regeneration groups – Bethnal Green City Challenge, East London Partnership, the Hackney, Deptford and North Peckham task forces plus three Training and Enterprise Councils.

The first chair was Sir Alan Shepherd of Grand Met. A subsequent chair was Archie Galloway of City Corporation whose position meant he could be impartial on route options. Outside expertise was needed and came from Michael Schabas[80] from Canary Wharf, and supported by Steer Davies Gleave, a leading transport consultancy. From 1993, policy and political support came from Jonathan Roberts at PR consultants Citigate; this was the same Jonathan Roberts who had been a key figure in the North London Line Committee. Lewisham Council initially paid for this and the cost was later spread across the group.

---

80 Canadian-born Schabas went on to found GB Railways which won the Anglia franchise, and which launched the first open access operator, Hull Trains.

Back at LRT, the ELLE working group was not to meet again until March 1992, while the government continued to pass the buck to cash-strapped London Transport for the absence of the extension. On 8 July, Viscount Astor, transport spokesman in the Lords, told questioners 'The government's position on the East London Line is quite simple: we await an appraisal from London Underground as and when it feels able to include the scheme in its investment programme'.

A few days later, the LUL board finally decided that it did indeed want to go ahead with the plan. The line would run from Highbury in the north to Peckham and East Dulwich in the south, and the trains would be the A class stock used on the line at the time. Network SouthEast would not support extensions further south, something which damaged the business case.

But it was an unpropitious time for transport projects. It wasn't just the anti-rail bias of the Thatcher and Major governments; high inflation since the mid-1980s had forced interest rates to high levels for sustained periods. They hit 10 per cent in July 1988 and stayed above that level for three years, peaking at almost 15 per cent. These were years of misery as small businesses collapsed under the interest rate burden and homeowners groaned under high and rising mortgage bills – in 1992 over 75,000 homes were repossessed by banks and building societies. In this climate, London and Edinburgh Trust's plan for Bishopsgate was shelved, and with it, any hope of a financial contribution to ELLE from that quarter.

On 16 September 1992 – Black Wednesday – the government's economic policy collapsed when the pound was forced out of the Exchange Rate Mechanism.

LT were not entirely discouraged. On 14 October 1992, Denis Tunnicliffe, LUL's managing director, told the board that the new plan was to submit the scheme to the transport minister and either deposit a Parliamentary Bill in November 1992 or its planning order equivalent in early 1993; £4.9 million in funding would be set aside to support this. With LET out of the picture and no other developer in sight for Bishopsgate, the expensive but useful Central Line interchange station was out. But there would be 'passive provision' for this in the future although it would 'have to be externally funded'. The project cost was now estimated at £98 million.

Against the grim economic background, Norman Lamont's financial statement in November (his last as chancellor) contained swingeing cuts in the settlement for London Transport. Planned investment of £1.39 billion would be cut to £1.01 billion in 1993, £1.19 billion in 1994, and £0.95 billion in 1995/96. Spending on roads, however, was untouched by the cuts.

On 3 March 1993 Tunnicliffe told the LT board that even though ELLE had 'attracted ministerial support', it had been 'made clear that there will be no additional government funding' for the extensions. Later that month, LT wrote to all London MPs spelling out the cuts. The East London Extension project was put on hold until 1996/97 at the earliest. As part of the cuts, the Underground's Aldwych and Ongar branches were slated for closure – which took place in September 1994.

LT doggedly continued with its plans. Now, LUL envisaged that the scheme 'would be taken forward as a joint venture with the private sector'. That is, it couldn't pay it for all itself and knew that the government wouldn't pick up the bill either. With the onset of privatisation, it wasn't even clear whether LUL would keep the project. It could easily become a through route for main line trains similar to Thameslink, serving outer suburban main line destinations. This would boost commuter access to Canary Wharf but might be at the cost of an all-stations inner London service designed to aid regeneration of these areas.

On 30 November, (the day of the 1993 Budget) LUL asked the government for an order under the Transport and Works Act 1992 (TWA) to give it the powers to build the extension plus four new stations – Bishopsgate, Hoxton, Haggerston and Dalston Junction.

The TWA was in theory a sensible idea, which allowed the minister to approve transport schemes in person, instead of forcing the promoters to apply for an expensive and time consuming private parliamentary bill, as BR had been forced to do in order to get the Liverpool Street redevelopment approved. On 11 October 1994, the planning inquiry began, under inspector Richard G Brown.

Brown heard that the cost of ELLE was likely to be £83 million. With a 30-year life and an assumed discount rate of eight per cent, the project had a net present value of £64 million and a benefit to cost ratio of 1.7 to 1 (which Brown called 'a good rate of return, especially for a public transport scheme').

There were 37 objections; mostly minor and often from local councils who firmly supported ELLE in principle. Great fairness was shown to individual objectors: the portrait photographer from Holywell Lane, Shoreditch who was concerned about vibration affecting his specially built darkroom; the Middleton Road, Haggerston couple who ran a musical instrument repair business where instruments were adjusted to high acoustic standards and who were worried by the potential noise; the small businesses who would lose their premises in via-duct arches, either temporarily or permanently.

Hackney Council tried to raise the uncertainty of funding, claiming it could 'delay the start of the scheme because of uncertainties for potential investors', but Brown sidestepped any comment on this highly political point. But he had no difficulty in approving the project, saying 'The overall economic and social benefits … are so great that the secretary of state might wish to look forward to early implementation of the scheme.'

By June 1995 it was announced that an £83 million Private Finance Initiative (PFI) scheme was under consideration to pay for the line. The PFI was a device invented by John Major's government to pay for public sector projects. It amounted to financial engineering – the key point being that the public does not actually own the asset delivered in its name. Instead, the authority makes an annual payment to the private company which provides the building and associated services, rather like a mortgage.

Meanwhile, transport department civil servants reviewed Brown's decisions on some objections and asked for further representations. And so it wasn't until 20 January 1997 that then transport minister Sir George Young made the order which gave permission to build ELLE.

In December 1997, with New Labour now in charge, John Prescott, Blair's minister responsible for transport, asked LT to prepare a report on the options for extending the East London Line. On 15 June 1999, when announcing the start of public private partnership (PPP) negotiations between Railtrack and LUL over the future of the sub-surface lines, Prescott confirmed that his proposals would incorporate extensions to the East London Line. The result would have been to integrate all these lines into the national rail network.

Although negotiations with Railtrack were broken off on 30 November, Prescott gave the go-ahead for discussions between Railtrack and LUL on the future of ELLE to continue, together with the SRA, and in December that year, the SRA invited bidders to submit investment proposals making use of the East, North and West London Lines. Yet it did not include these routes in its next round of franchise negotiations.

On 17 March 2000, LUL made up its mind about the southern terminus of ELLE. It applied to build extensions on to Railtrack lines in south London, with services to Wimbledon, Croydon and Crystal Palace. Railtrack, which would benefit from track access charges, was naturally far more sympathetic to this idea than Network SouthEast had been.

Bishopsgate, meanwhile, remained derelict. With no development on the horizon, Railtrack, as the privatised successor to the BRB, gave – on 5 April 1998 – a 10 year lease to Spitalfields Space Management and Cityside Regeneration for them to use the vast spaces underneath the arches at Bishopsgate for smaller businesses including those displaced from the Spitalfields Market development. A go-karting arena and tennis courts would also be provided.

And still the question remained, after 10 years of hard work by ELLG – who was going to pay for the extension? Part of the answer came – four years into the life of the Labour government – on 2 April 2001 when the Strategic Rail Authority announced the first tranche of funding – to the tune of £39 million – for land purchase, design and development work on the northern extension. This wouldn't pay for the building of the line – but it was a start, and was enough to keep the project going. The SRA's Strategic Plan, published in January 2002, planned for the SRA to let the concession for the extension later that year, and control of works would then pass to the concessionaire.

A February report to the TfL board[81] noted that the SRA intended to 'roll forward' £11 million from the transport department's overall allocation to the SRA for the project, into 2002/03 to allow it to continue beyond the initial works stage. The plan was that later in 2002, the SRA would let a Design, Build, Finance and Maintain concession contract – a PFI – for the main construction. The SRA was finalising the business case for the project with help from TfL.

One issue was train length; the existing East London Line could only handle four-car trains but as the plan was to extend this line on to the national rail network, the idea was to develop the line for eight-car trains and this option was evaluated in the business case.

Just when things seemed set to go, a bizarre legal dispute managed to add two whole years to the project. The row revolved around the only technically difficult part of the scheme, the linking of the East London with the old North London viaduct. The plan was to abandon the section of the East London Line into Shoreditch LT station, and instead, divert from this on a steep 1 in 30 gradient, to cross the Great Eastern main line via a new bridge and continue in a north-westerly direction to cross and demolish part of the unused Bishopsgate site. It would then continue via a new bridge over Shoreditch High Street and another over Holywell Lane to join the abandoned North London Line viaduct. This itself entailed the demolition of the remaining pieces of the Broad Street viaduct over Holywell Lane.

The plan ran into legal opposition from a tiny group of railway enthusiasts organised in the London Railway Heritage Society, who were determined to save the entire Bishopsgate goods yard site. They had discovered that LUL was now in technical breach of one of the covenants in the deemed planning permission it had acquired when the government approved LUL's TWA request in 1997. And so they went to court.

LUL warned that the time needed to make a new application and environmental assessment would effectively 'kill the project' because the government was unlikely to make a favourable decision on continued funding.

A critical part of the Bishopsgate site was the so-called Braithwaite Viaduct, named after the engineer of the Eastern Counties Railway who had designed it in 1840. It was thus one of the earliest structures of its kind in the world. In March 2002, the Braithwaite Viaduct had been listed by culture secretary, Tessa Jowell. But now, English Heritage was calling for the entire Bishopsgate site to be listed saying that 'needless demolition of the Bishopsgate goods yard would be a conservation tragedy'. This was a complete reversal of its position at the 1994 planning inquiry, when it had said there was 'nothing of special architectural or historic interest' other than the gates and screen wall that were already listed at the time.

---

81   TfL Board Papers, 5 February 2002.

English Heritage commissioned a report from structural engineers which claimed that the viaduct was still sound enough to carry rail traffic, and it proposed that ELLE go over this viaduct, so avoiding demolition and damage elsewhere. LUL was not impressed, replying that 'engineers believe that it is not safe to run a railway over these structures'. If they could not demonstrate to the Railway Inspectorate that the structures are safe then 'the extension would not go-ahead'. LUL insisted that it only needed to demolish part of the goods yard.

Prince Charles then waded into the row. On 29 April he complained about what he called 'genetically modified urban planning', saying 'Surely there must be a way to use the character of these historic arches to reinvigorate this unique part of London. Do we', he asked, 'Want to destroy one of the City's astonishing hidden treasures and replace it with another conventional office development?'

The small businesses and occupiers of the goods station were issued with notices to quit on 9 May. The go-karting arena closed the following month after opening the previous year.

On 8 November, Mr Justice Ouseley in the High Court agreed that LUL was in technical breach of the planning agreement but passed the buck as to whether LUL needed to apply afresh for planning permission. He said 'I express no conclusion as to whether LUL can or cannot lawfully demolish all of the goods yard that it wishes to, regardless of whether or not the 1997 permission has lapsed. It is for the planning authorities to decide what to do if LUL start to demolish the unlisted parts of the goods yard. The way in which they react or fail to react may be subject to review in the courts.'

So it went back to Hackney and Tower Hamlets and while they considered their position, the work was stalled. The East London Line Group replied with a glossy brochure warning of the threat to the line and quoting Livingstone, who said 'Any unnecessary delay would be disastrous'.

On 27 February 2003, Tower Hamlets decided to keep their nerve. They would take no action on the planning breach on the grounds of expedience and public interest. Its lawyers had warned councillors that the council faced another legal challenge, which could be costly if it lost, if it failed to enforce action on LUL. But the council and its planners realised that this issue would completely derail a project which was central to regeneration plans, and decided to stand firm. Hackney soon followed Tower Hamlets.

The enthusiasts went back to court for a declaration that the two councils were behaving illegally in not taking enforcement against LUL. On 2 May, Mr Justice Collins firmly rebuffed them. He agreed that the authorities should have made conditions for the preservation of the Braithwaite Viaduct but ruled that Hackney and Tower Hamlets councils were right in not opposing LUL's proposal to demolish much of the site, even though its planning consent had expired.

By July the TfL board was told that the SRA-funded preparatory works were

The old NLR bridge over Kingsland High Street.

continuing: 'whilst the project is being reviewed against a number of concerns. These included cost escalation from £0.6 billion in April 2001 to £1.3 billion in April 2002.'

On 14 July 2003, demolition began to make way for the future Bishopsgate station – now to be known as Shoreditch High Street. English Heritage by this stage had confirmed that it was satisfied that the method of demolition would not in fact threaten the listed Braithwaite Viaduct.

In September, TfL and the SRA submitted the business case to ministers on the basis of Metro services running on to the national rail network. Next month, the TfL board noted that a unified project team had been set-up under a SRA project director. The SRA had funded the project for the next two years but its future was still subject to further negotiations. Discussions continued between the SRA, the transport department and the Treasury on a so-called Special Purpose Vehicle under the PFI to pay for building the extension.

ELLE was re-approved by the SRA investment committee on 5 November and by the SRA executive a week later. The SRA asked for government re-authorisation of the scheme and the SRA board agreed on 5 December that the ELLE could proceed – but only subject to ministerial permission.

Nothing happened.

ELLG complained: 'The project has stalled in recent months. The business case, which contains proposed service patterns and a funding plan, was submitted by the SRA to ministers in late summer, but has still not been signed off.'[82] And until then there could be no funding and no progress.

So by February 2004, and after 17 years of work, solid support from all stakeholders and no-one even opposed to it, the TfL board was told, glumly: 'It remains unclear whether government is presently committed to full funding of ELLE'.

---

82   ELLG evidence to Select Committee on Culture, Media and Sport, 10 January 2003.

2004–2014: 'A FANTASTIC MODEL'

In which we look at how Transport for London built Overground – a brand new, top performing railway – when it finally won control, and how the North London Line now thrives.

It is impossible to overestimate the importance of the 2012 Olympics when it came to the transport revolution on the North London Line. Ken Livingstone was to say 'I do not think there is any prospect that we would have achieved the decision to go ahead and extend the East London Line to Croydon, Crystal Palace and up into Hackney without the Olympics because it was in the bottom ten of the priorities of the Strategic Rail Authority'.[83]

He subsequently went much further, telling the *Daily Mirror*[84]: 'I didn't bid for the Olympics because I wanted three weeks of sport. I bid for the Olympics because it's the only way to get the billions of pounds out of the government to develop the East End'.

The Olympic victory was, in fact, heavily predicated on rapid and visible transport improvements in east London. There were only three schemes which could be delivered in time and it was these three which formed the core of TfL's strategy. The North London Line was central to each of them. They were:

1. Improve services and stations on the core North London Line.
2. Restore services on the viaduct north to Dalston and on to Highbury by building the East London Line Extension.
3. Replace North London Line services east of Stratford with Docklands Light Railway trains.

All these were made possible because the 2004 financial settlement allowed TfL to borrow on the international money markets. As a government institution with a secure revenue stream from fares it was a good credit risk, currently AA+ at Standard & Poors for example. Borrowing on the money markets meant TfL could avoid the tyranny of the Private Finance Initiative, which, although invented by the Conservatives, was continued by Labour as its preferred way of paying for major projects while keeping the cost off the nation's books. Instead, TfL went looking for funding – and found it in Luxembourg. In September 2005, three months after London won the fight to host the 2012 Olympics, the European Investment Bank signed a low-interest £450 million loan to TfL.

The Commons Treasury sub-committee was later to hear some damning evidence from Steve Allen, TfL's managing director, finance, about how PFI really worked, evidence which fully justified its determination to leave the scheme well alone. Allen explained that because TfL could borrow directly, it could

---

83   Evidence to Select Committee on Culture, Media and Sport, 1 November 2005.
84   *Daily Mirror*, 24 April 2008.

accurately measure what PFI really provided in value for money terms. The conclusion? 'Although TfL's cost of borrowing is probably something to the order of between 0.5 per cent and 1 per cent above gilt rates,' it was still cheaper than using PFI. He concluded, 'I think it is hard to say that if you look across all the projects, overall PFI is value for money against that additional cost of finance'.

Ian Brown, a career railwayman who became managing director of TfL in 2007 and who had worked on ELLE from its start, later said it was fortunate not to have to be funded through the 'nightmare' of PFI funding.

We can look at the last of the three improvement projects first – the ending of North London Line trains east of Stratford. The genesis of this scheme was back in 1998, when John Prescott proposed extending the DLR to provide a connection between the existing station complex at Stratford and the planned new Eurostar station at Stratford International, on the north side of the Great Eastern main line.[85] As the existing DLR tracks from Poplar were on the *south* side of the main line, feasibility studies suggested that the best approach was to use the North London Line low-level platforms and track to burrow under Stratford main line station. This meant handing over the NLL tracks south to Custom House to the DLR, which fitted in with the continuing regeneration proposals for this area.

By February 2003, TfL already had approval to extend the DLR into the Royal Docks, and so Network Rail sought approval to shut the North London Line east of Stratford, with Canning Town, Custom House, Silvertown and North Woolwich stations closing. The conversion to DLR would cost £111 million, including more trains for the DLR.

Traffic statistics presented a not very cheering picture. From 2002–03 to 2005–06, traffic at North Woolwich had risen by 76 per cent to 118,000 passenger arrivals and departures a year. But similar figures for Custom House showed a decline of 12 per cent to 66,184 and at Silvertown of 49 per cent to just 24,765 on the same period. Only eight stations in London now had less traffic than Silvertown. In 1987 the station had been renamed and partially rebuilt as Silvertown and London City Airport. However, the infrequent service and depressing walk through back streets meant that few passengers came this way.

By comparison, the 2005–06 passenger figures for Hackney Central were 513,943, for Camden Road 688,609 and for Dalston Kingsland 821,557. Clearly there was little further growth to be expected on the eastern section.

The new branch of the DLR from Canning Town to a new station in North Woolwich called George V would duplicate the North London Line and provide a more frequent service to more destinations, including the City and eventually, under the river to Woolwich. Consultation – involving open days

---

85   TfL Board agenda, May 2005.

Silvertown station a week before closure.

and leaflet drops to 70,000 residents – was overwhelmingly positive, and when, after DoT approval, TfL applied for closure, there were only 32 objections, with most being settled in advance of the inquiry.[86] The last train left North Woolwich on Saturday night, 9 December 2006 and North London Line trains were then diverted into new high-level platforms at Stratford.

86   A 2008 survey carried out by Social Research Associates for DLR, found that 74 per cent of respondents in North Woolwich felt that the DLR had improved things for them personally. A study in 2006, before the DLR opened, revealed an area characterised by a poor self image, with low expectations for jobs and educational achievement as well as a growing lack of community cohesion.

A September 2011 visit to the area showed the 1979 North Woolwich station still visible, with the entry closed up, through the metal fencing, while the old station – which achieved Grade II listing in 1998 – was now boarded up with metal shutters, and signs warning that all valuable material inside it had been removed. It closed as a railway museum after cash-strapped Newham Council couldn't support it any more. Plants were growing from the pediments and some of the upper windows have already been smashed. The track has now been lifted and the entire track bed is now in the hands of Crossrail which will be using it for the Abbey Wood branch.

The platform and building at Silvertown were still intact, with the trackbed featuring piles of old sleepers. Here and there a length of sunken track still crossed Factory Road, the last evidence of the numerous sidings which once served factories in the area.

The second Olympic project, building the East London extension, didn't depend on the expiry of the Silverlink franchise; work could start as soon as the project was handed over to TfL and so we should consider this next. The scheme was an obvious winner:

- With an estimated cost of £800 million, it could be completed at a fraction of the price of other major rail schemes which would enhance an Olympic bid.
- As it mainly involved existing structures such as the City Link Viaduct, it could be completed within a relatively short timeframe. TfL's 2002 annual report reckoned that the opening of the line could be achieved by 2008. So unlike other major projects, ELLE could be open well in advance of the 2012 Olympics.
- And ELLE had almost universal support from London and national stakeholders.

The old terminus at North Woolwich ... boarded up and abandoned.

The handover to TfL in 2004 meant that ELLE now had a serious sponsor, and the first phase of the project – north to Dalston Junction – was duly included as part of the TfL five-year investment programme unveiled by Livingstone on 12 October. The second phase would terminate at Highbury – proposals to extend ELLE trains over the Canonbury curve, were abandoned by the SRA for operational reasons, probably because they would need frequent trains coming from the East London Line to (1) cross the North London tracks on the level, (2) use Canonbury tunnel which, as we have seen, was now singled, and (3) would have required this section electrifying into Finsbury Park on the DC system, where there was a shortage of platform capacity and no obvious place to reverse trains.[87]

Since the closure of the Dalston to Broad Street section over 20 years before, decay had set in on the viaduct, and making this fit for rail traffic again was the first job to be undertaken. In June 2005, the preparatory work on the viaduct began, led by Taylor Woodrow, and this went on to the end of 2006. This involved, apart from the new stations:

- Refurbishment of 210 arches. Three of these, near Haggerston, were in such a bad state that they needed to be demolished and replaced with a concrete structure allowing more space for the station entry.
- Waterproofing of the entire structure and vegetation clearance.
- Repointing of brickwork.
- Replacing 22 bridges. A number of the plated steel girder structures were found to be in an advanced state of deterioration and needed replacement. Since the underbridges were of sub-standard headroom clearance, collision protection beams were fitted to all.

In October 2006, TfL awarded the main construction contract, worth £363 million, to a Balfour Beatty and Carillion joint venture for rebuilding the entire line between Dalston Junction and West Croydon. The scope involved the replacement of 4.5 miles of track, installation of signalling equipment on the Whitechapel to New Cross stretch, building 2.2 miles of new trackbed from Whitechapel to Dalston Junction and four new stations at Shoreditch High Street, Hoxton, Haggerston and Dalston Junction. To further benefit these deprived areas, TfL took the tendering process further than had ever been done previously by specifying the employment of local workers and putting in place ways of monitoring compliance.

The London boroughs and communities involved were ecstatic that this project was now finally going to happen. The East London Line Group claimed that building the line would be the catalyst for £10 billion worth of economic regeneration with patronage on the line itself likely to increase by 300 per cent by 2021. The specific benefits were claimed as:

---

87 Proceeding to Finsbury Park had been ruled out by London Transport's East London Steering Group back in December 1989.

- Cutting congestion on the existing rail network, especially on journeys to London Bridge and the Northern Line (via Bank), and to Waterloo, Victoria and the Thameslink stations.
- Reducing journey times from outer London to Docklands, the City and other parts of inner London.
- Promoting orbital rail services, reducing the need to interchange and so relieving congestion at central terminals.
- Improving public transport access to poorly served areas including parts of Docklands, Hackney, Lambeth, Lewisham and Southwark.
- Meeting the growing demand for railway services, making full use of a valuable river crossing in east London.
- Relieving road congestion, especially the South Circular, the roads through Lewisham and the Rotherhithe Tunnel, and the New North Road and Kingsland Road to Aldgate by giving a rail alternative.

But not quite everyone was happy. From a trade union point of view, all this looked like privatisation and unions launched a campaign to warn that well-paid and secure jobs with London Underground would be outsourced to cheaper private companies.

Despite his 'Red Ken' sobriquet, Livingstone took a pragmatic view against his left wing and union critics, calling them 'unrealistic'. He said – pointedly writing in the *Morning Star* – 'The deal is not exactly as I would have liked it – I would prefer the new Overground to be fully in public ownership. But the government is not going to hand over sections of the national rail network to me so I can nationalise them. That was never an option, unfortunately'.[88]

He added: 'The extension of the East London Line has always been a national rail project. This was originally to be taken forward by the Strategic Rail Authority. However, as there was little sign of progress over some years, I successfully argued for the government to transfer the project to TfL'.

Ian Brown told *Tribune*[89], another left wing newspaper: 'There will be absolutely no redundancies and all current staff will be offered alternative positions with London Underground in full consultation with the trade unions'. Undeterred, on 23 October 2006, RMT general secretary Bob Crow, TSSA assistant general secretary Manuel Cortes and TUC southeast regional secretary Megan Dobney were to be found at Canada Water and other stations urging East London Line users to tell Livingstone to scrap 'privatisation' plans.

Regardless of the union protests, the contract for operating the entire Overground project was let on 2 July 2007. It went to an MTR (which operates the Hong Kong Metro) and Laing Rail joint venture for a seven-year concession with a two-year potential extension. The defeated bidders were Govia, National Express Group and Nedrail. The successful company was swiftly renamed

---

88 *Morning Star*, 20 October 2006.
89 *Tribune*, 14 July 2006.

London Overground Rail Operations (LOROL). The Laing Rail share in LOROL was subsequently sold to Arriva, a subsidiary of Deutsche Bahn.

The concession listed eight measurable objectives. They included improving the passenger experience (quality of stations, security, train performance and reliability), increasing revenue, introducing new rolling stock, integrating the East London Line into the system and a 2012 Olympics plan.

The railway would be operated as a 'concession', not a franchise. Network Rail would continue to manage the infrastructure and LOROL would run the services. TfL would set the fares, decide service levels, buy and manage the trains and take a hands-on approach to decision making, exactly as it did with the Docklands Light Railway. In return for taking more operational control, TfL would pick up the overwhelming majority of the revenue risk – up to 90 per cent of it. This made the operator's books much easier to manage and their profit margins clearer, a worthwhile payoff for tighter working restrictions.

Meanwhile, Livingstone was making progress in solving another headache for London travellers – getting the privatised train operators in the capital to accept the Oyster card. An outline agreement for them to accept pay-as-you-go was signed on 31 January 2007. The caveat was that the London taxpayer had to pay for this. Livingstone had already offered to provide £20 million to help pay for the provision and installation of smartcard readers, station equipment and back-office support systems.

As part of the Oyster roll-out, special pink card readers were installed at some interchange stations to give Overground travellers the benefit of cheaper travel when the route avoided the central zones. Highbury to Gunnersbury for example cost £1.60 at peak times and £1.50 offpeak on the North London Line compared with £3.20 and £2.70 on the tube through zone one.[90]

On 12 November 2007 Livingstone was able to stand on the platform at Hampstead Heath and announce the birth of London Overground to the assembled media. Officially, the newly-formed company had taken over the Silverlink franchise the day before, but it was here that Livingstone laid out his vision for the future of the NLL and beyond – a clean, reliable, trusted, orbital service.

Back in the East End, Shoreditch LT station had closed for the last time on 9 June 2006. On 22 December 2007 the rest of the East London Line closed for complete rebuilding to main line standards. A series of rail replacement buses was provided to link the stations on the line, but they didn't cross the river due to height restrictions in the Rotherhithe Tunnel. The cutting to Shoreditch station was subsequently filled in to create more open space in the area, and the small station building on Pedley Street was locked up and abandoned to the vandals. Five years later – in February 2011 – it was sold at auction for the surprisingly high price of £665,000.

---

90   Figures correct at February 2014.

On the northern extension, progress was starting on the heavy bridgework. Over the Christmas period, the old bridge over the Great Eastern main line into Bishopsgate yard was removed to make way for a new bridge at a different angle. On 29 March 2008, a new bridge weighing 350 tonnes was lifted into place – to cheers of watching spectators – over Shoreditch High Street. The 84 metre bridge was manufactured to a bowstring design by engineering firm Fairfield Mabey of Chepstow, transported in segments, and assembled on the Bishopsgate Goods Yard site. This bridge has become a real border marking the transition from post-industrial Shoreditch to the skyscrapers of the expanding City just beyond. This is by design and not accident; both City and Hackney wanted the bridge to have a gateway visual presence and the steel tied-arch bridge was chosen instead of a cheaper concrete structure for this very reason.

On 4–5 May, Liverpool Street station was closed to allow a 1,300 tonne Warren truss bridge carrying the extension across the Great Eastern Main Line tracks to be installed, with the engineers inching it slowly into place on the same kind of wheels used to manoeuvre space shuttles to their launch pads. TfL installed webcams so the progress could be followed online. The bridge launch itself was successful, but on 28 May, the bridge dropped 200mm on to its permanent supports as it was being jacked down. Debris fell on to the tracks, forcing the suspension of services in and out of Liverpool Street station until the following day and causing major disruption to commuters.

The new stations illustrated the centrality of the property development industry to the new line.

Shoreditch High Street is the showpiece. It serves an area very different from the run-down dereliction which so upset councillor Roberts in the early 1980s. Its low-rise Victorian workshops, long abandoned by industry, have been converted to a variety of bars, restaurants, art galleries and urban loft apartments. On an old section of the North London viaduct between Holywell Lane and Great Eastern Street, four disused and graffiti covered tube train carriages perch high above the ground, providing yet more space for artists' studios. The area is now the very epitome of 'urban cool'.[91]

Into this low-rise landscape, Shoreditch High Street station was a large concrete box made of precast panels. it is a highly striking example of modern brutalism – the radical architectural critic Owen Hatherley described it as: 'A huge concrete warship smashing into the old Bishopsgate Goods Yard'.[92] But in fact the station design was entirely functional: the idea was not to protect passengers from the rain but to protect the track from the debris of the building site which might grow up around it if ever the rest of Bishopsgate is developed. Without this concrete box, substantial interruptions to the service would certainly be required once development began.

---

91   It is actually 'outcooled' by Dalston, described by the Italian edition of *Vogue* in April 2009 as the coolest place in Britain.

92   http://urbantrawl.blogspot.com/2011/03/east-london-line-extension.html

'A huge concrete warship' – Shoreditch High Street station.

However, Shoreditch High Street was in zone one, even though the old Shoreditch LT station was in zone two. A Freedom of Information Act request uncovered the fact that TfL had been forced to rezone by the transport department as a condition of providing £24 million of funding for the final link in the Overground network, from Surrey Quays over the South London Line to Clapham Junction. The DfT was anxious to protect revenue for the South Central franchise.[93] To mitigate the effect, TfL promised a special local fare for passengers travelling between Dalston and Wapping so they would be charged as if they all their journey were in zone two.

Hackney Council wants to make a virtue of the Shoreditch box. Its planning guidance for the site noted that it was visible in the view looking south from the corner of Chance and Old Nichol Streets in the South Shoreditch conservation area, adding that development of the goods yard should seek to preserve or enhance this view from the conservation area.

93   http://www.londonreconnections.com/2009/an-east-london-line-foi-request/

In 2002 with Railtrack on its last legs, the remnants of its property portfolio – including Bishopsgate – were sold for £63 million to Hammerson. Although Hackney was prepared to accept tall buildings on its part of the site, Hammerson gave a five-year lease of a small part of the site to the innovative Shoreditch Boxpark, a shopping mall in converted containers. Hammerson and Ballymore are pressing ahead with their £800 million project for Bishopsgate. PLP is to design the first stage which will feature 2,000 homes, while FaulknerBrowns will oversee retail space which will integrate with the Braithwaite viaduct. A high-level public park above the viaduct could provide up to 1.7 hectares of open space similar to the famous New York high line park.

The Hoxton station, all steel and glass, with plenty of protection from the elements at viaduct level, is slightly misnamed, being on the wrong side of Kingsland Road. It is a brand new station – no passenger facilities existed here in pre-1923 North London Railway days – although it is actually on the site of the former Dunloe Street goods depot. Its entrance is within a series of the existing (and impressively restored) brick arches and the architect was Weston Williamson. The south ends of the platforms provide a spectacular view of the City at night.

Northbound train nears Hoxton with the Gherkin, Cheesegrater, and NatWest Tower in the background along with the tower of St Leonards Shoreditch.

Haggerston is immediately to the north of the original NLR station. The chosen design from Acanthus featured towers in conscious imitation of Holden's stations for the Piccadilly Line extension of the 1930s. The station features a Tod Hanson-designed public artwork piece based on Haggerston-born astronomer Edmond Halley of comet fame.

The new Dalston Junction (more stainless steel panels and again by Weston Williamson), generated some unrest locally as it was designed to fit in with the regeneration of Dalston town centre, which involved Barratt, the housebuilder, getting permission to build two large tower blocks which were overwhelmingly for private sale. A local pressure group – Open Dalston – alleged that the regeneration project had led to the demolition of a number of historic buildings, which had been allowed to decay by the council, in order to allow TfL to build a white elephant bus station above the station.[94] All this required that the new station was essentially underground in order that something could be built above it and so that the line could be extended on to the NLL.

There is something startling that, after the rooftop ride from Shoreditch and its opportunity to observe the ever-changing cityscape in this part of the capital, the line suddenly descends (at 1 in 43/44/45 all the way from Haggerston) into darkness. Hatherley called it 'a grim, low canopy akin to those inserted in the 1980s under the office blocks of Charing Cross or Liverpool Street'.

Dalston Junction has a wide island platform, the outer sides providing through services, with two central bays supporting terminating services from both New Cross and West Croydon. The route eastward – the eastern curve – is protected for possible use by the planned Crossrail 2 by ensuring that the piles to support the development above the station are positioned to support the restoration of the route if ever required. The land above this has become a popular community space – the Dalston Eastern Curve Garden,[95] featuring a wooden garden pavilion for events, and workshops. Trees and shrubs were planted alongside butterfly bushes, bracken and other plants which were already growing on the derelict site. Sadly this urban oasis is now under threat from a proposed expansion to the Dalston shopping centre.

All of the stations have been provided with lift access to help disabled passengers.

Meanwhile, phase two of ELLE – to link up with the North London Line and terminate at Highbury – had been approved. Bringing this into being required huge works to the North London Line, and it is to this final part of the Olympic strategy we must now return.

When TfL took over from Silverlink in 2007, they put great emphasis on visible, quick-win type improvements. The stations were quickly rebranded as Overground with a version of the LT roundel – but with an orange instead of

---

94   *Private Eye*, 10–23 August 2012.
95   See http://dalstongarden.org/

Hampstead Heath, 2007 – the Overground launch with Ken Livingstone (left) and Peter Hendy and Ian Brown of TfL (right).

a red circle. It was based on the colour used for the East London Line since 1990 and it was this colour which was adopted and extended for the entire Overground network. Short-term, the Silverlink branding on the trains was quickly covered up by a London Overground sticker.

Stations started to be staffed again, with 120 new jobs being created in the process. Within a year, all stations had received a comprehensive deep cleaning to get rid of dirt and chewing gum. Ticket halls, floor markings, lamp posts, handrails, stair-risers and fences were repainted to help visually impaired passengers; guttering was cleared, years of graffiti removed. Public address, CCTV, information displays and lighting were all checked and repaired and anti-pigeon roosting measures were installed. Further work was planned to renew all station systems by the end of 2010. Passenger gates were progressively installed which reduced the intimidating atmosphere at night, as well as increasing revenue; these gates helped cut journeys made without valid tickets from ten per cent to three per cent within a year of TfL control, and by November 2011 the figure had fallen to just two per cent. With more trains and passengers about, and a real perception that someone now cared, the vandalism and graffiti did not return.

On the border – the Overground bridge marks the transition from low-rise Shoreditch to high-rise City.

To run a better service, TfL needed to get rid of the 313 class trains, and use brand new trains designed specifically for the needs of the line and its customers. TfL started its procurement competition in mid-2005: for the East London Line, bids were received from suppliers of new-build rolling stock, and cascaded Class 458 stock was offered of the type used on the south-western lines from Waterloo. But this was not considered suitable and would have needed significant refurbishment. Also, TfL wanted a single fleet, and there were not enough 458s for the North London Line as well.

Three full bids were received, from Bombardier, Hitachi and Siemens. In the end, the TfL order went to Bombardier for 44 Electrostar 378 trains to be built at Derby at a cost of £223 million. Twenty-four dual voltage three-car trains were ordered for the North London section with the aim of getting them into service from late 2008. Twenty DC-only four-car trains were ordered for the extended East London Line. These were based on units operating successfully on the southern suburban lines; but the lesson of the old 313 stock was thoroughly learned; all seating was longitudinal and wide gangways were employed to make it possible to have more standing passengers. This was an inevitable compromise – reducing seating for passengers travelling the length of the line who might have to stand for much of the journey. But this was considered acceptable because the average journey distance on the line is only 4.3 miles. This meant they provided 33 per cent more capacity than the old trains. Longitudinal seating also presented security advantages – any wrongdoing could be more easily captured on CCTV. Air conditioning was provided too. In July 2007, TfL placed a further £36 million order for an extra 36 carriages to allow the North London service to move to having four cars instead of three.

TfL doesn't own the trains; they are leased from QW, a joint venture between the National Australia Bank and Sumitomo Mitsui Banking Corporation. TfL said that the lease deal meant it could save £250 million of capital which could be reinvested. There would be no overall saving from leasing, but TfL would not bear the cost of the depreciating value of the fleet.

However, the plan to run eight trains per hour all day received a setback in August 2008 when it was decided to suspend the restoration of four-track operation through Camden Road station. This cut £40 million worth of costs, especially by removing the need for bridge repair work, and TfL claimed it would limit disruption to road and rail services in the area. The Railfuture pressure group complained about 'apparent major miscalculation of the extent of the costs and risks associated with the replacement of Bridges 71, 83 and 94'. There was also some grumbling from freight industry groups, and the plan for a terminal bay platform at Camden Road had to be abandoned as a result. This in turn meant that augmented services across the Stratford to Camden section had to be shelved as they would have to go on to the Primrose Hill line to reverse, where they would block freight.

That left eight trains per hour in the peak, and six off-peak. Of the six trains per hour, two would run over the West London Line, serving a new station at Shepherds Bush, to Clapham Junction. But this meant that the western section of the North London Line (Willesden to Richmond) saw less of the benefit of the upgrade and still has only four trains an hour. There were no plans to progress the idea of a Stratford to Queen's Park service.

Just before Christmas 2009, TfL announced the inevitable shutdown of services to allow for the upgrade of track and signalling, and the linking in of ELLE. The scale of the project was huge; £326 million would be invested in the rebuild with TfL paying 44 per cent, the Olympic Delivery Authority 32 per cent, Network Rail 23 per cent and the transport department one per cent.

From 20 February 2010, the line closed between Gospel Oak and Stratford to allow more than 200 signals, 4.5 miles of track and 69 sets of points to be improved and 30 station platforms lengthened to handle the four-car trains. The track through Hampstead Tunnel had already been lowered to allow it to take the W10 size container trains. There seemed little passenger grumbling – the fact that such drastic closures were needed might, paradoxically, have given passengers confidence that – at long last – something really was being done, especially as the scale of the work was visible to anyone who cared to look.

The Highbury and Canonbury areas were revolutionised. The passenger platforms for the old No 1 (AC) lines were restored at both stations and the North London Line services were diverted on to these, sharing them with the freight traffic. Highbury acquired a new overbridge at the west end of the station. The southerly ex-DC lines, meanwhile were handed over to the ELLE trains. Both stations were equipped with lifts to allow access for disabled passengers; Highbury was thoroughly improved, although the unsatisfactory interchange with the Victoria Line was not touched at all. The miserable station buildings at Canonbury were retained but the platforms were cleaner and brighter, although there were no canopies installed, and no covered way to the platforms either. The decision to abandon the four-tracking plan to Camden left Caledonian Road with a curious layout; the old westbound platform was taken out of service, a fence was installed, and the existing eastbound platform was converted to an island layout to handle trains in both directions, meaning that all passengers now needed to use the overbridge or lift.

At Stratford, the old NLL low-level platforms were given over to DLR trains, and a brand new high-level pair of platforms was built as part of the comprehensive rebuild of the station executed as part of the Jubilee Line extension, which together with more DLR trains, made Stratford into a critical interchange point. Elsewhere, re-extending platforms which had been reduced in the 1960s was one of the main engineering headaches. Dalston Kingsland and Willesden High Level were probably the worst problem cases. At Dalston, already a cramped site, Boleyn Road had to be completely reconstructed to allow the existing platforms to be extended westwards. At Willesden the situation was worse still. Previous bridge reconstruction work had widened the bridge where the North London Line passes over the Watford DC lines, but in doing so had removed part of the platform. This had to be restored so that four-car trains could be handled.

Services resumed between Stratford and Richmond on 1 June 2010, at first with three-coach trains. These were extended to four cars in the spring of 2011. At the end of 2010, the remaining signal boxes (Dalston Western Junction, Camden Road, and Gospel Oak) were closed and control of the line shifted to the centre at Upminster.

Test runs on the East London extension began on 5 October 2009, and on 27 April 2010 a limited 'preview' service began between Dalston Junction and New Cross/New Cross Gate, and the line came into full operation between Dalston and West Croydon/Crystal Palace on 23 May. Full services to Highbury began on 28 February 2011, two months ahead of schedule.

At the time of writing, there are eight trains an hour between Highbury and the southern destinations with others running between the bay platform at Dalston Junction and New Cross. Highbury and Canonbury now have a service every few minutes, meaning that this section enjoys a tube-like quality of service.

Ironically, Livingstone, who had done so much for London travellers, had lost office in the 2008 mayoral elections and the opening ceremony was performed by his Conservative successor, Boris Johnson. Caroline Pidgeon, a Liberal Democrat member of the London Assembly, sourly commented: 'Right in the middle of a general election campaign, the mayor is desperate to claim credit for something he didn't initiate'.

The rebuilding of the North London Line was indeed a triumph – one which stands as a shining example of what can be achieved and which is a standing rebuke to much of the privatised railway system. The success was reflected in increased passengers and a superb punctuality and reliability record – one which is almost unrecognisable to those who suffered in the Silverlink days of the late 1990s.

Passengers grew from 0.6 million journeys per week in 2007 to almost two million journeys in September 2011 and these are now two and a half times the level when TfL took over in 2007. A large part of the growth came from the extended East London Line – but the existing Overground network also experienced an increase in demand of 80 per cent.

Taken as a whole, London Overground carried 135.7 million passengers in 2013/14. This was 4.9 per cent above target, and represented a year-on-year demand growth of 8.9 per cent. This increase was the largest clocked up by any part of the TfL empire.

A look at station usage statistics for a selection of stations over the past provides a breakdown of the traffic growth[96] (see Table nine, page 168). Data quality is somewhat variable – for example travel using Oyster pay as you go has been included from January 2010. Previously, Oyster pay-as-you-go journeys were not included in station usage figures, and this caused a notional increase in the figures for 2010–2011. The dips in 2008–2009 were caused by the TfL takeover, which meant journeys were switched to travelcards rather than tickets bought from the train operators, as well as the impact of the line closures for refurbishment. Even with these caveats the big picture is clear enough: table nine shows that for the selected stations – and taking into account data quality issues – entries and exits were up by an average of 69 per cent between 2011 and 2013, with the two Hackney stations showing increases of over 70 per cent!

The official rail usage figures provide comments for particularly large year on year changes. For the North London Line they included 'continuing ramp-up of London Overground travel' and 'further improvements to Overground service including completion of link between north and east branches in February 2011 driving continued large increases in demand'.

During this period, rail travel had increased nationwide, but relatively, it was growing much faster on the North London Line. This can be shown by table ten (page 169) which tracks the climb in the ranking of a sample of NLL stations when ranked by total number of exits and entries. By 2012–13, Dalston Kingsland and Hackney Central had become two of the top 100 most used stations in the UK. Highbury & Islington is ranked at 27th nationwide; it is unclear how much of this traffic is from the North London Line, but probably quite enough to make it a top 100 station just on North London Line traffic.

---

96   Source – Station Usage Data – Office of Rail Regulation (Delta Rail).

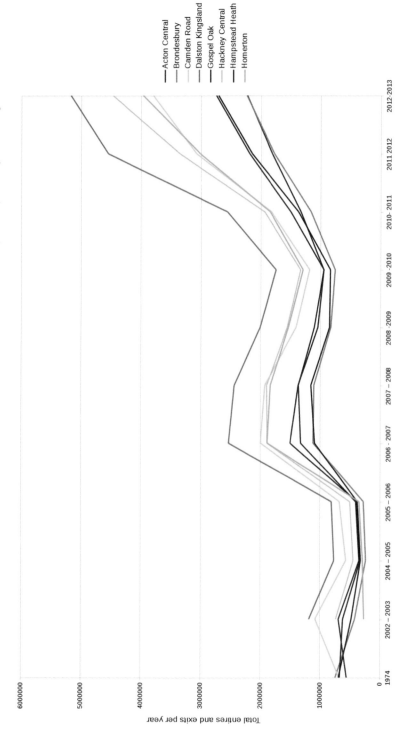

Table nine: the passenger explosion - 1974-2003

Source - Office of Rail Regulation. (1974 figures based on BR passenger census for one week with figures extrapolated to give 52 week figure

Table ten – usage ranking of selected North London Line stations

Station	Rank 2002–2003	Rank 2010–2011	Rank 2011–2012	Rank 2012–2013
Dalston Kingsland	232	165	79	75
Camden Road	267	256	138	107
Hackney Central	364	232	119	83
Acton Central	408	351	275	227
Gospel Oak	439	314	223	170
Homerton	748	251	141	102
Hampstead Heath	530	341	227	172
Brondesbury	596	400	285	224

Punctuality and reliability have steadily increased too. By Period 11 of the 2012/13 year, the Overground PPM figure was 96.7 per cent. It had dropped below 95 per cent in only one period in the preceding two years.

The independent Passenger Focus survey for August 2012 gave Overground a 93 per cent satisfaction rating – in joint second place out of all operators – and eight points ahead of the London and South East average. The *Which?* train satisfaction survey put Overground at the top of the commuter rankings and second in the overall category behind Virgin.

Table eleven – London Overground PPM: 2008–2013

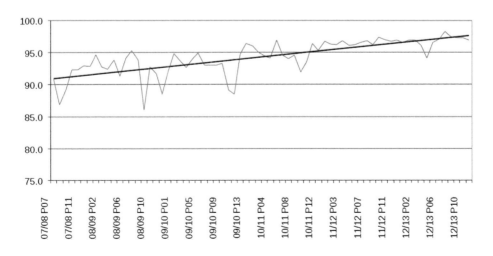

In May 2012, TfL transport commissioner Peter Hendy said 'The Overground is a fantastic model. I don't think anybody expected the transformation of the Overground to be half as successful as in fact it's been. And the reason for that is because we've correctly recognised it's an urban railway serving Greater London in a similar way that the tube serves it, and that some of the same conditions that you would then apply are the ones which greatly generate income. Like staffed stations. Like a frequent service. Like attractive stations.'

It seems highly unlikely that the line would have boomed had BR remained in charge. There was what John Sanderson calls 'a complete lack of ambition' surrounding the line, and its managers were themselves battered from years of cutbacks and underfunding. BR didn't really know what to do with the line and it would never have been able to bring the marketing focus that TfL achieved. David Kirby of BR London and South East even told the LRPC in 1985: 'Personally I don't think railways are very suitable for orbital journeys. Our *raison d'être* has got to be improving journeys to central London.' In 1977 BR executives doubted whether journeys at Kentish Town West could ever hit 500,000 a year; they are now running at over three times that figure!

The amazing growth in traffic highlighted the central flaw in the Beeching plan, which called for disinvestment in infrastructure without knowing what would be needed in the future. The Save The Broad Street Line (Hampstead) Committee said way back in 1964: 'Losses, real or alleged are irrelevant, for losses belong to the past and the present – BR have not the remotest idea of what the total traffic and transport movements are going to be in 10, 20, or 30 years time'.

And paradoxically, the controversial closure of the Broad Street link was the making of the modern railway. Even though the motive for the closure was property development, and it was vigorously opposed by transport campaigners, Chris Austin may well be right when he says that the closure 'forced the line to focus on being a truly orbital route'.

North London's tradition of community and environmental activism continues today. A group of local residents helped set up The Friends of Homerton Station, which has created a wildflower meadow on the embankments supporting this very urban station. The group plants wildflowers, runs fortnightly tidying up and weeding sessions and has a poster working group to commission posters from local artists for display inside the station.

The future for passengers on the North London Line will be dominated, just as it has been for the past 20 years, by the question of capacity. London's population is expected to continue to grow, hitting 8.3 million by 2026. It was rising population, together with economic revitalisation in inner London, which led to the traffic boom in the 1990s and further growth looks certain – London has weathered the post-2008 recession much better than other parts of the country. The TfL lobbying strategy consistently points to the centrality of London's economy when arguing for continuing investment in the capital – sometimes in

The new look at Highbury, taken from the 2011 footbridge.

16 April 2013, a well used off peak service showing the interior of the new trains.

the face of provincial resentment; and TfL warned: 'Due to the lead times for providing new rail capacity, it is necessary to act before the levels of crowding become so severe that they choke off employment growth and damage London's business efficiency and contribution to the UK economy'.

Providing a better service has encouraged more passengers to use it, and there is no doubt that longer and more frequent trains will be required if overcrowding is not to return and undo much of the good work done since 2004.

TfL measures overcrowding by the number of standing passengers per square metre of standing space. Extrapolating from today's traffic figures and growth, TfL predicts – by 2021 – 'severe levels of crowding,' defined as 3–4 people per square metre, between Willesden Junction and Acton, doubtless reflecting the fact that this section has only four trains per hour with uneven intervals (10/20/10/20), and 'significant crowding' (2–3 people per square metre) between Hackney Central and Camden, Gospel Oak and Hampstead Heath, and between Acton and Gunnersbury.[97] Gunnersbury station in fact already experiences serious crowding at peak hours and its small and dismal booking hall and entrance is really due a comprehensive rebuild. Individual trains may experience significantly worse overcrowding than the average, of course.

In July 2011, TfL's submission for the next financing round called for five-car running to contain overcrowding. Longer trains provide more scarce capacity without having to squeeze more trains into the congested timetable. The context was HLOS2[98] – which would set out the key objectives and projects which the government wanted to see completed for Britain's railways in the period 2014 to 2019.

For the entire Overground network, moving to five-car trains would mean buying or leasing another 130 vehicles and this has a lead time of around two years from contract signing to Bombardier delivering. The total investment in orbital routes would be £310 million with an annual increase in operating costs of £21 million.[99]

There may be scope for some extra PiXC buster trains to be inserted into the schedules at peak hours. At present, the signalling provides for 12 trains per hour, both passenger and freight, in each direction. With freight trains essentially prohibited from occupying peak hour paths, the passenger service is stuck at six trains per hour off-peak and eight trains at peak hours, and some small improvements may be possible. During the Olympics, when six million passengers were carried on the overground network, eight trains an hour were run all day, which gives a glimpse of the service theoretically possible, but only on the basis of removing almost all daytime freight traffic from the lines, which is unrealistic.

---

97 The very worst crowding, classified as 'very severe crowding' will be found on the West London and South London lines, and on the East London line from Forest Hill to Canada Water.
98 For High Level Output Specification.
99 The submission also included within this figure the electrification of the Gospel Oak to Barking route and running four-car trains on it instead of the two-car trains currently in use.

A September 2012 timetable adjustment removed the annoyance that trains were reverting to a 30-minute frequency far too early at night. Previously, if you missed the 22.36 eastbound from Camden Road you faced a 30-minute wait as the next train wasn't until 23.06. Highbury could do with a simple 'first train to Canonbury and Dalston' indicator, while a 'first train to Highbury' indicator would be very useful at Canonbury.

A notable omission from the TfL HLOS submission was a service from Stratford via Primrose Hill to Queen's Park. From TfL's viewpoint, today the issue with the Queen's Park service is that it would be a zero sum game; operating every train on that route means one fewer train via Gospel Oak which TfL regards as the 'main line'. A service via Primrose Hill doesn't exist at the moment and TfL capacity modelling suggests that capacity is better used on the service via Gospel Oak. A related problem is surely that this scheme may have been linked to the ending of Watford line DC trains to Euston and, in turn, the extension of Bakerloo line trains from Harrow to Watford. But this latter scheme is 'on hold indefinitely due to funding and business case constraints'.[100]

However, when transport minister Justine Greening announced the contents of HLOS2 on 16 July 2012, there was no mention of the words 'Overground' or 'Transport for London' in the entire document. Why is unclear. One explanation is an (as yet) submerged political row over who should pay for the continued improvements needed when transport is devolved as in the case of TfL or Merseyrail. When Jeremy Corbyn, MP for Islington North, asked why the Gospel Oak to Barking line had been left out of the list of lines to be electrified, Greening replied that it was a matter for TfL. Greening lost this job shortly after the announcement, due to her opposition to expanding Heathrow Airport.

But TfL pressed ahead with longer trains, with funding for this written into the TfL business plan in late 2012. Formal approval for a £320 million spend was given in January 2013 for five-car trains to run on the East London section by December 2014 and the North London a year later. But even with this latest spend, rising passenger demand will mean overcrowding will still remain 'significant' between Dalston and Camden, Gospel Oak and Hampstead Heath, and between Willesden and Acton. The LOROL concession meanwhile was extended for two more years to November 2016.

Work to extend platforms to support five car trains began in spring 2014 on the east London section, which will be the first to receive the longer trains. Some weekend closures will be required for this work. Nowhere on the north London section will need to use selective door opening (SDO) – that is, keeping one set of doors closed due to short platforms – which delays trains as passengers need to shuffle along the carriage. But the impossibility of extending platforms at Wapping and Rotherhithe means it will definitely be needed there.

100 *Croxley Rail Link – Value For Money Annex Report*, Steer Davies, Gleave, 2011.

SDO will also be needed at the very busy Canada Water interchange where the East London Line crosses the Jubilee Line Extension. The use of prefabricated platform extensions should limit the need for service outages – weekend closures might be involved but not ones of weeks or months. In some cases signals may need to be moved if they are currently positioned too close to the end of the platform. The very busy stations at Dalston Kingsland and West Hampstead will present different problems in a five-car world – although longer platforms can be planned in, there may be the need for secondary entrances as both stations were designed with ticket halls for considerably less traffic than is now achieved. Dalston has only three automatic gates, for example, with one more for disabled passengers.

Howard Smith, former chief operating officer at TfL, says there are 'no active plans' for a Central Line station at Shoreditch High Street. TfL estimates that the cost would now be around £100 million. The main value would be to allow Overground users to change on to the Central Line to get to the West End, but the Crossrail interchange at Whitechapel – just one station on – would bring much the same benefits once Crossrail opens in 2018. Of course, when a developer is finally found for the Bishopsgate site, it might still view a Central Line interchange as being important. Whether it would be important enough to pay some or all of its construction costs remains to be seen.

Another currently dead project is the proposal to restore four-track operations through Camden Road. On 25 November 2008, the Labour government announced another £1 billion investment in transport, of which £54 million was earmarked for this post Olympics. But TfL now says there is 'no prospect' of this work going ahead. Howard Smith says 'It doesn't do very much, it would only shift the pinchpoint to the other side of Camden Road station', adding that a lot more useful benefit could be obtained from that level of spend.

Further station improvements however are ongoing. The next tranche of access schemes includes installing lifts at Hampstead Heath, Brondesbury, Kensal Rise and West Hampstead, while they have already been installed at Camden Road, Gospel Oak and Hackney Central, paid for by the transport department's Access for All Programme.

A strategic interchange will be built in Hackney, linking Hackney Central on the North London Line, with Hackney Downs. Such a link existed in the Victorian era and today the road link is used by 150,000 people a year. Restoring it will cut the transfer time from 14 minutes by road to just five minutes along a covered walkway and passengers won't need to go through ticket barriers either. The walkway will be somewhat limited – it will connect the westbound North London Line platform at Hackney Central with platform 1, used by southbound trains, at Hackney Downs. But the scheme will not feature the original 1870 station building, which now hosts a Nordic-themed restaurant and nightspot. Hackney Council approved the planning application in February 2014 with completion scheduled for 2015 at a cost of £5 million.

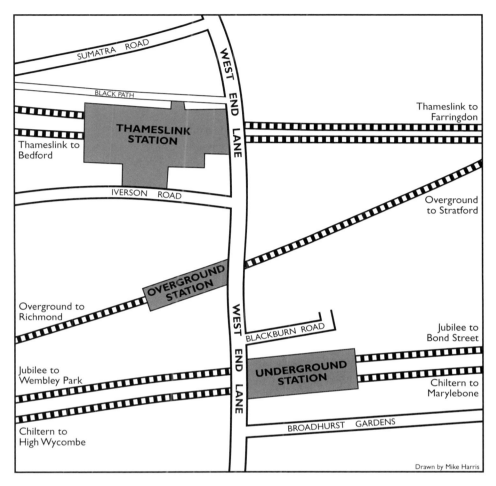

Improving the unsatisfactory interchange between the North London, Thameslink and Jubilee Lines at West Hampstead has been the subject of many proposals over the years. The three stations adjoin each other on West End Lane, but that for the Jubilee Line, the most southerly of the three, is on the opposite side of the street, and narrow pavements and busy traffic generate a very sub-optimal interchange.

In 1999, Railtrack applied to redevelop the land to the west of West End Lane for a mixed-use development consisting of new Thameslink and NLL stations and mixed residential, retail and leisure use. Camden Council wasn't happy, raising a variety of concerns, especially that the proposals would not provide a substantial improvement to the integration of the stations. TfL carried out a study two years later to work out 'whether there was a realistically fundable and deliverable scheme to integrate the three stations'. In January 2003, it concluded that no such scheme existed, and recommended that improvements to an on-street interchange should be pursued instead.

In 2002, Chiltern Railways came forward with a redevelopment proposal for an interchange at West Hampstead with new platforms for its Marylebone to Birmingham trains. It would be paid for by mixed-use high-density development. This plan was dropped when Laing Rail, which owned Chiltern, became involved in the TfL takeover of Silverlink.

Network Rail went ahead with a new Thameslink station, which opened on Iverson Road late in 2011. This did improve the interchange – but a fully integrated station on this difficult site seems as far off as ever.

Faced with the continuing demand for freight train paths, TfL's strategy has been to push as much of this traffic away from London as possible, and a dedicated rail strategy document was produced in 2007,[101] and incorporated into the Mayor's Transport Strategy document of 2010. And significant amounts of money are now being spent upgrading the cross-country route from Felixstowe, via Ely, Peterborough and Leicester onto Nuneaton, to take W10 size containers. Some of this money came from the port operators at Felixstowe and Harwich whose traffic will benefit most. This will include, when completed, a new curve at Ipswich, and restoration of double-track working in the fens between Ely and Soham. These two projects, costing £41 million, increase capacity between Ipswich and Peterborough from 10 container trains a day to 24 per day. Another £40 million project provides a new track and bridge across the West Coast Main Line at Nuneaton so freight trains can proceed north without crossing the existing lines on the flat. As a result, fewer freight trains from Felixstowe and Harwich need to travel to the north through London, so making space for a more frequent passenger service.

As against that, there will be two new contenders for scarce access rights. One, which is certain, is freight traffic from the new 1,500 acre deep sea port being built at London Gateway on the former Shellhaven refinery site in Essex. Traffic from here to the north will need passage through north London and the logical route will be over the Barking to Gospel Oak line and then over the North London Line to Willesden. In 2007, the government approved £18.5 million of funding towards the capacity and gauge enhancement of Barking to Gospel Oak, following an application from Network Rail and TfL.

The electrification of this line was finally agreed in 2013 as part of the Government's ambitious rail investment plan. The cost was given at £115 million, which includes the connections to various main lines, and this will not be completed until at least 2017. The 2014 Budget announced that the route would be extended to serve Barking Riverside, a post-industrial zone where London's largest housing project is stalled because of non-existent transport links. Electrification will take some pressure off the North London Line, but not all; freight from the London Gateway port will still need to use the Gospel Oak to Willesden section.

---

101 Transport for London: *Rail Freight Strategy*, August 2007.

A further threat to Overground was dramatically removed in March 2014 when it was decided to scrap the proposed connection between the fast link to the Channel Tunnel (HS1) and HS2, the proposed fast line to Birmingham. HS2 is planned to start at Euston and travel underground through north-west London. But a link was planned from HS2 onto the North London Line viaduct near Primrose Hill. This would have allowed Eurostar trains which can already join the North London Line above St Pancras to pass onto HS2.

The link would have needed seven bridges to be rebuilt or extended with closures being required to achieve this. It would also have needed four-tracking to be restored through Camden Road.

HS2 originally claimed that: 'Initial work suggests that services on the North London Line will not be significantly affected', but mayor Boris Johnson – re-elected in May 2012 – opposed the link from the start demanding: 'Alternative options must be identified that do not adversely impact on London's rail services. The proposed link would largely use existing tracks and would adversely impact London Overground capacity and performance.'

A March 2014 cost-cutting review by HS2's new chief executive Sir David Higgins, a former boss of Network Rail, accepted that the link was 'an imperfect compromise' which would also use up capacity on HS2 which could be used to run more services to areas such as north Wales.[102] It would have cost £700 million to build – even considering inflation this seems a vast amount of money considering that the rebuild of the North London Line only cost £326 million. The Government immediately agreed that this wasn't value for money and promised to scrap the link.

However the HS2 plan includes a vastly expanded Euston station, which will inevitably take years to build. So there is still the question of whether the DC service to Watford can continue in an expanded Euston or whether it will have to be finally diverted to Stratford – or even, via a new link, onto Crossrail. Challenged on this in 2012 TfL said: 'There is no indication that (HS2) will have implications on current services.'[103]

So that concludes our tour round 25 miles or so of railway and over half a century of transport politics and history. We have seen how a Cinderella line could escape closure due to well-organised protest, and how also it exploded in popularity once management and control were transferred to people with a vision of what needed to be done with it and resources were made available to let them deliver. The figures speak for themselves; any further comment from me would be superfluous.

---

102 HS2 Plus, a report by David Higgins.
103 *Brent and Kilburn Times* 20 January 2012.

SOURCES AND ACKNOWLEDGEMENTS

Many people helped me with this study and their time and effort are gratefully acknowledged. Jonathan Roberts and Jim Connor kindly read through the draft, made useful comments and provided leads for further enquiries. Any errors which remain are of course my own.

Thanks also are due to others who spent time with me and were generous with their recollections and/or loan of documents. They include Chris Austin, Peter Staveley, Stephen Joseph, Howard Smith, Roger Blake, John Sanderson, and Roger Lansdown. Stephanie Rousseau at TfL corporate archives helped dig out files regarding the tortuous story of the East London Line Extension.

Credit goes to Transport for London who make board meeting documents freely available on their website.

The American radical campaigner Michael Moore once termed librarians 'footsoldiers of democracy'. Without the London Metropolitan Archives, Camden and Islington public libraries, Guildhall reference library in the City and the National Archives at Kew, this book would not have been possible.

Introduction
- Robbins, M. *The North London Railway*, first published 1946 with several editions following.

1945–1960: Picking up the pieces
- National Archives. For the post-war closures of Hammersmith, Poplar, Kew Bridge and Olympia services, see AN 13/1681, AN 13/880, and AN 13/1355.
- London Metropolitan Archives. Records of the Transport Users Consultative Committee under the series LRPC.

1962–1965: 'This troublesome matter'
- National Archives. For closure proposals AN 155/33 and for the related transport ministry files see MT 124/699.
- London Metropolitan Archives. Records of the Broad Street – Richmond Joint Committee and the local Hampstead committee, series A/BSL and A/BSH.
- London Metropolitan Archives. Records of the Transport Users Consultative Committee under the series LRPC.
- Save the Broad Street – Richmond Line (Hampstead Committee) *Hampstead and the Broad Street Line*, 1964.
- London Borough of Islington libraries. Local history collection – press cuttings from the period.
- Austin C, and Faulkner R. *Holding The Line*, 2012.

1965–1968: 'Absolute minimal facilities'

- National Archives. For the reconstruction of the line after reprieve, see AN 155/33 and for Grant Aid and the Broad Street to Watford service see AN 155/251 and AN 155/252. For the demise of the Poplar Dock branch see AN 169/11 and AN 156/136, while the Freightliner story as it affects north London is at AN 115/237, AN 201/10, and AN 199/546.
- Kitchenside G. *The North London Line Today parts one and two*, Railway World April 1967 and June 1967.

1968–1985: 'Financial Anarchy'

- London Metropolitan Archives. For GLC involvement and the extension of the service eastwards see GLC/DG/ADG/05/027 and GLC/DG/ADG/05/028 and GLC/TD/TP/POL/10/963.
- London Metropolitan Archives. Archives of the North London Line Committee. Series B97/101 but currently uncatalogued.
- National Archives. GLC involvement and relations with central government are at AN 176/85 and AN 188/87. The Kentish Town West affair appears at AN 176/44 and AN 176/110 and AC freight electrification at AN 199/164 and AN 199/165.
- Crowther G L, Vickers P H, Pilling A D. *A new Ringrail for London*, 1973.
- Greater London Council and Department of Environment. *London Rail Study, parts one and two*, 1974.
- Greater London Council (planning and communications policy committee). *Proposed electrification of the BR line from Dalston to North Woolwich*, 1981.
- North London Line Committee. *Save the North London Line*, 1974.

1979–1985: 'Not as reliable as we would have liked'

- Perren B. *Third Rail to North Woolwich*, Modern Railways, October 1984.
- North London Line Committee. *Hackney Line Diesel Services*, 1978.
- National Archives. AN 188/87 and MT 198/3.

1971–1986: 'Half forgotten and half destroyed'

- National Archives. For the redevelopment of Liverpool Street and the controversy over the fate of Broad Street and North London Line trains, see AN 184/461, 463, 464, 468, 469, 472, 473; AN 199/483, 484, 485; AN 188/72, 99, AN 192/173, and MT 124/1335.
- Jackson A A. *London's Termini*, 1966, second edition 1972.
- Rosehaugh Stanhope Developments and BRPB. *Broadgate*, 1985.
- Hackney Public Transport Action Committee. *The case for Shoreditch Church Station*, 1981.

- London Regional Passengers' Committee. *Report into proposal by the British Railways Board to close the line between Dalston Western Junction and Broad Street*, November 1984.
- Hackney Public Transport Action Committee. *City Link: the case for the railway*, 1984.

1986–1992: 'Grotesque figures indeed'

- Bancroft P. *Broad Street – death of a station*, London Railway Record, January 1995.
- National Archives. AN 18/1456 and AN 211/154 for the Liverpool Street to Watford service.

1983–2007: 'Shabby, unreliable, unsafe, overcrowded'

- London Assembly. *London's forgotten railway*, 2005.
- Network Rail. *Route Utilisation Strategy – cross-London traffic*, August 2006.
- Network Rail. *Route Utilisation Strategy – freight traffic*, March 2007.
- London Borough of Hackney. *Response to Network Rail's draft cross-London route utilisation strategy*, 2006.
- Design for London. *Heritage audit of the London Overground, vols 1,2 and 3*.
- Harris M. *Investment in North London*, Modern Railways, February 1994.
- Harris M. *NSE north division takes stock*, Modern Railways, May 1993.
- London Passenger Transport Committee. Annual reports.
- London Borough of Islington. *Islington and the Union Railway – submission to Union Railways consultation on Channel Tunnel Rail Link*, 1993.
- London Metropolitan Archives. Minutes of the LPTC and its various subcommittees under the series LRPC.
- National Archives. AN 211/45, AN 211/162, AN 200/287, AN 18/1596, AN 167/58 and AN 211/164 for impact of the Channel Tunnel fast link, AN 199/546 for freight impact, AN 188/303 for the NSE 1992 Rail Plan.
- London Borough of Camden libraries. Local history collection – press cuttings from the period.
- London Borough of Islington libraries. Local history collection – press cuttings from the period.
- Hamnett C. *London: unequal city – London in the global arena*, 2003.
- Network SouthEast (North Division). *Expanding the Horizons*, 1993.
- Lawrence M. *Network Southeast – from sectorisation to privatisation*, 1994.
- North London Line Committee. *Submission to Union Railways consultation on Channel Tunnel Rail Link*, 1993.

- South Caledonian Community Association. Papers of Randall Keynes (King's Cross Railways Lands Group) in London Borough of Islington archive.
- Huntingdon Street/Crescent Street/Thornhill Square Union Rail Action Group. *Union Rail's proposals affect the quality of your life and the value of your property*, 1993.

1987–2004: 'The East London Connection'

- Transport for London Corporate Archives. The frustrating story of the East London Line Extension appears among the series LT001965/004.
- Ove Arup. *East London Assessment study*, 1989.
- National Archives. AN 184/514, AN 184/519, AN 184/520, AN 167/1216 and AN 167/1242 for the BRPB redevelopment plans for Bishopsgate Goods Yard.
- Harris N. *East London Line – where next?* Modern Railways, May 1996.
- Bray, J. *East London Line Extension*, Modern Railways, October 1992.
- Roberts, J. *An Enduring legacy, the East London Line Group 1990–2010*, 2010.
- Schabas M. *East London Line Extension, statement of case, East London Line Group*, 1992.
- East London Line Group. *Orbital Rail and Outer London*, 2009.

2004–2014: 'A fantastic model'

- London Connections blog at http://londonconnections.blogspot.co.uk. – (sadly defunct but still archived) An indispensable source for observers of London's transport scene is John Bull's very much alive www.london-reconnections.com/website.
- *Open Dalston* http://opendalston.blogspot.co.uk.
- Friends of Homerton Station http://www.friendsofhomerton.org.uk.
- Network Rail. *Route plans 2009, route 6 – North London Line and Thamesside.*
- Transport for London. Board agenda papers and minutes 2000–2012.
- Transport for London. Rail and Underground Panel minutes – http://www.tfl.gov.uk/corporate/about-tfl/boardandchiefofficers/papers/1444.
- Transport for London. *TfL recommendations for the High Level Output Specification for 2014–2019 (HLOS2)*, July 2011.
- Transport for London. *London Overground Impact Study*, November 2011.
- Transport for London. *Response to Network Rail's Draft Cross-London Route Utilisation Strategy.*
- Transport for London. *Business Plan*, December 2012.
- Whitelaw J. *East London Line Reborn – Major Project Report*, New Civil Engineer, 27 May 2010.

INDEX

ILLUSTRATION CREDITS

Wayne Asher: 110, 155, 161, 164, 171.
Mike Ashworth: 71.
Ian Baker: 107.
Tony Bock: 53.
Ben Brooksbank: 43, 86, 121, 141.
Matt Buck: 137.
Tom Burnham: 78.
Capital Transport: 17, 160, 171.
Nick Catford: 140, 154.
Dr Neil Clifton: 151.
ColourRail: 54, 137.
Justin Cormack: 133.
Gordon Edgar: 98.
John Furnevel: 100.
Getty Images: 19.
Stacey Harris: 75.
Nico Hogg: 114.
Kevin Lane: 64, 108.
Henry Law: 101.
Rob Macspite: 51.
Colin Marsden: Cover, 66, 82, 97, 125.
Museum of London/Roger Mayne: 31.
National Media Museum: 90.
NS&I archive: 23.
Andrew Panatti: 63.
Railway Review: 20.
Jonathan Roberts: 5.
John Sanderson: 127.
Mike Slocombe: 135.
Southern Region BR: 63, 79.
Transport for London: 163.
Nigel Wood: 73.